HAVING FUN TOGETHER

CREATIVE IDEAS FOR FAMILIES

DEBBIE STAPLEY

HAVING FUN TOGETHER

CREATIVE IDEAS FOR FAMILIES

Bookcraft
Salt Lake City, Utah

Library of Congress Catalog Card Number: 92-72655
ISBN 0-88494-837-4

First Printing, 1992

Printed in the United States of America

To my parents, Don and Virginia Sedgwick,
for their trust in me as a child
and for the example they are to me still—

And to Greg, Amanda, Rebecca, and Elissa,
for their love, patience, and putting up with
an untidy house every once in a while.

Contents

Acknowledgments

Special thanks to Candace Smith for introducing me to Bookcraft, for her encouragement, and for allowing me to use her "Birthday Party for Your House" idea in my book.

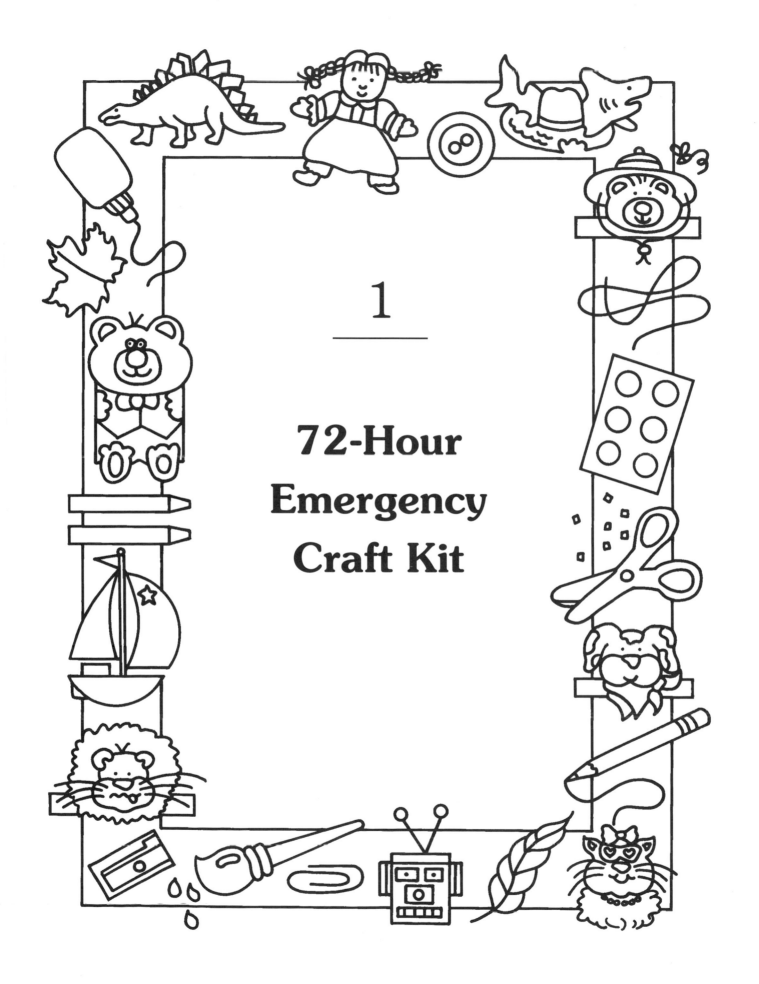

1

72-Hour Emergency Craft Kit

72-Hour Emergency Craft Kit

Whether it is summertime or the middle of the winter, children can be struck by that ugly disease, the "I'm Bored" syndrome. This chapter outlines all of the materials needed to make a craft kit that will keep children busy for months, and provides instructions for twenty fun and inexpensive craft ideas using the materials in the kit. If you will take an hour or two to put it together, nobody will be happier than you that you have it.

Step 1: Find an old suitcase (or buy one from a thrift store).

Step 2: Accumulate the items on the Materials List.

Step 3: Put the materials inside the suitcase.

Step 4: Copy the Crafty Instructions from this chapter and place them inside the suitcase with the materials.

Step 5: Hide the craft kit and use it only for emergencies.

Materials List

Newsprint roll end (available wherever newspapers are printed and costs about two dollars for hundreds of square feet)
All-purpose white glue—one for each child
Squirt guns
Construction paper, typing paper, and plain white paper
Thick paper towels
4 or 5 glass medicine droppers
4 or 5 baby food jars
Paper lunch sacks
Markers, crayons, and pencils
Popsicle sticks
Large paper grocery sacks
Old magazines
Fabric, felt, and yarn scraps
Glass wax (available at grocery stores)
Feathers
Wide tape

Poster paint and acrylic paint
Straws
Plastic spoons
Disposable saucers
13-by-9-inch pan (old and/or disposable)
Pre-pasted wallpaper scraps or samples
Sandpaper (fine and coarse)
Magnetic tape
Scissors
Cardboard or poster board scraps
Large-eye plastic needle
Hole punch
Old-fashioned clothespins
Chenille stems (pipe cleaners)
Paintbrushes
Plastic pill bottles
Jar of odds and ends (buttons, coins, glitter, and so forth)
Cardboard egg cartons
Cellophane
Old toothbrush
String
Spray paint

Crafty Instructions

Crazy Hats

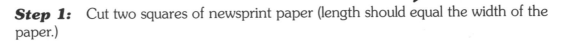

Materials needed:

Newsprint paper
Watered-down white glue (use three
    parts of glue to one part water)
Paintbrush(es)
String or yarn
Spray paint

Step 1: Cut two squares of newsprint paper (length should equal the width of the paper.)

Step 2: Quickly paint the surface of one paper square with the watered-down glue and set the other paper square on top of it. Press out all of the air bubbles with your hands.

Step 3: Drape the "glue sandwich" on top of a child's head, and carefully tie a string around the circumference of the head.

Step 4: Gently lift the paper off of the head and set it on the floor. Cut and shape the hat's brim into any configuration you want and then let it dry.

Step 5: Have the child paint the hat, and then wear it.

Suggestions for hat designs: Buccaneer, witch, flower, straw (actually glue straw to the outside of the hat instead of painting), cowboy, or crazy (anything goes).

 This is a great activity idea for a child's party—not to mention Halloween!

Life-Size Self-Portrait

Materials needed:

>   Newsprint paper
>   Markers or crayons
>   Scraps of yarn, felt, fabric, feathers, paper, and
>   so forth
>   Glue

Step 1: Cut a piece of newsprint paper one or two feet longer than the length of your child.

Step 2: Have the child lie down while you trace her outline onto the paper.

Step 3: Have your child decorate her paper body with clothes made from fabric scraps and hair made from yarn. Encourage her to use her imagination and turn herself into something fun, such as a clown or astronaut!

Squirt Gun Art

Children have a lot of fun with this activity, but they do need to understand the rules before you give them the "loaded guns."

Materials needed:

>   Newsprint paper
>   Squirt guns
>   Wide tape

Thinned poster paint (use one part paint, one part soapy water; adding some dish soap to the water before using it to thin the paint will help clothes, hands, and anything else the paint comes in contact with come clean)

Step 1: Dress your children in old clothes.

Step 2: Use the tape to hang large sheets of newsprint paper on the wall of your garage or anyplace else that might easily be hosed down. Tape some paper to the floor also to make cleanup easier (this activity can be messy).

Step 3: Fill squirt guns with watered-down paint and let your children go to town—on the *paper*, not the car, the bikes, or the lawn mower.

Drop Painting

Materials needed:

Food coloring
Baby food jars (one for each color desired)
Droppers (one for each color desired)
Thick paper towels

Step 1: Fill baby food jars with water (not quite to the top). Add about ten drops of a different color of food coloring into each jar of water.

Step 2: Cover a table with a vinyl table cloth or several layers of a newspaper. Set one thick paper towel in front of each child.

Step 3: Using droppers, have the children drop the "paint" onto the paper towels, one drop at a time. The drops will fan out and bleed into each other, creating a very pretty picture. Children will be happy to make what is essentially the same picture over and over again because making it is so much fun.

Sand Pictures

Materials needed:

Salt
Food coloring
Plastic cups or glasses
Watered-down white glue (use two parts glue to
    one part water)

Paint brush
Coarse sandpaper

Step 1:   Put about 1/4 cup of salt into each cup (one for each color desired).

Step 2:   Drop a different color of food coloring into each cup and mix it with the salt.

Step 3:   Have the children paint the sandpaper with watered-down glue, then sprinkle the sandpaper with the different colors of salt. Tap off the excess.

Have them try painting the inside of a jar with the glue and layering different colors of salt in it, creating a sand painting in a bottle!

Wallpaper Bead Necklaces

Materials needed:

Large bowl or 13-by-9-inch pan
Scissors
Pre-pasted wallpaper samples or scraps (free samples are
    available from hardware or wallpaper stores)

Step 1:   Cut wallpaper into triangles.

Step 2:   Fill bowl or pan with water and wet all the triangles.

Step 3:   Starting with an edge of the triangle (not a point), roll up each triangle and let it dry.

When dry, the rolled-up triangles will be hard and your children can use them like beads to make necklaces, bracelets, or other jewelry.

Leaf Printing

Materials needed:

Leaves from the outdoors
Thin paper
Crayons

Step 1:   Have the children arrange different leaves on a sheet of paper.

Step 2: Place another sheet on top of the leaves and tell the children to color the top sheet.

Step 3: If your children are old enough, have them try to find the names of these plants by identifying the leaves in an encyclopedia.

Skeletonized Leaves

Materials needed:

    Leaves from the outdoors   Old toothbrush
    1 teaspoon baking soda   2 tablespoons bleach

Step 1: Boil leaves in a solution of 1 teaspoon baking soda and one quart water for 1/2 hour. Leave them in the solution until cool.

Step 2: Remove leaves from the solution and place them on a piece of paper.

Step 3: Gently brush away the fleshy part of the leaves with a toothbrush.

Step 4: Soak the leaves in a solution of 2 tablespoons bleach and 1 quart water for 1 1/2 hours. Press the skeletonized leaves in a book.

Egg Carton Creatures

Materials needed:

    Cardboard egg carton   Glue
    Chenille stems   Paint
    Cellophane   Construction paper

Step 1: Cut a piece of the egg carton to use as the creature's body.

Step 2: Poke holes into the egg carton and insert chenille stems for legs, arms, and antennae.

Step 3: Glue on pieces of cellophane or construction paper for wings and then paint as desired.

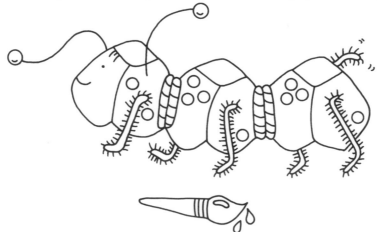

Pill Bottle Pendant

Materials needed:

Plastic pill bottles (without the lids)
Pennies, glitter, marbles, beads, a piece of crayon, or anything else that might fit into the bottle

Step 1: Set the oven to 450 degrees.

Step 2: Place a small object into the pill bottle and set it on a foil-covered pan.

Step 3: Put the pan in the oven for about ten minutes or until the bottle has melted.

Step 4: Remove the pan from the oven and let it cool.

Step 5: Drill or pierce a hole in the pendant, and attach it to a chain or length of yarn.

Clothespin Doll

Materials needed:

Old fashioned clothespins
Glue
Fabric scraps
Chenille stems
Yarn, cotton, or fringe
Sandpaper
String
Acrylic paints
Paintbrush

Step 1: Sand off enough of the bottom of the clothespin to make it stand up.

Step 2: Paint the face, and glue on yarn, cotton, or fringe for the hair. Let it dry.

Step 3: Fold a chenille stem in half and twist the ends together. Bring the twisted end together with the folded end and press it flat. This piece will make up the arms. It should be *about* the same length as the clothespin.

Step 4:   Wrap a scrap of fabric around
the chenille stem, leaving a little bit of each
end (the hands) sticking out. Glue it in place
on the back of the clothespin.

Step 5:   Copy the pattern shown here for
the shirt (you may need to alter this pattern
to fit your clothespin), or make up your own
pattern. Cut the shape out of the fabric, and
run the arms through the holes in the shirt.

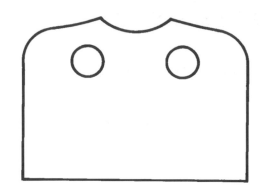

Step 6:   Wrap the shirt around the doll
and glue it in place.

Step 7:   Cut a 3-by-5-inch piece of fabric.
Tie one long end to the waist of the doll, as
shown in the diagram.

Step 8:   Embellish the doll as desired,
adding aprons, ties, bows, and other acces-
sories with glue.

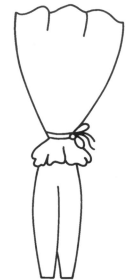

Sewing Card

Materials needed:

       Old magazines or colored pictures from coloring books
       Cardboard scraps
       Yarn
       Large-eye plastic needle
       Glue or spray adhesive
       Hole punch or hammer and awl

Step 1:   Using glue or spray adhesive,
attach a picture from a magazine or coloring book to a piece of cardboard.

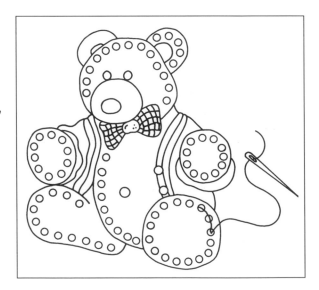

Step 2:   Punch holes in the picture
with a hole punch or hammer and awl.

Step 3:   Thread the needle with the
yarn and let your child "sew" in and out
of the holes.

Puzzle

Materials needed:

Old magazines or colored pictures from a coloring book
Cardboard scraps
Glue or spray adhesive
Scissors or craft knife

Step 1:   Using glue or spray adhesive, attach a picture to a piece of cardboard.

Step 2:   Have your children create a puzzle by cutting the pictures into various shapes with scissors or a craft knife.

 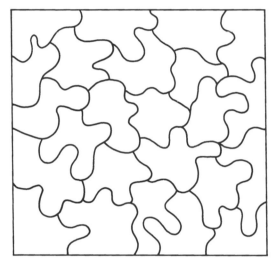

Create a Story

Materials needed:

Old magazines	Scissors
Construction paper	Cardboard or poster board scraps
Glue or spray adhesive	Magnetic tape

Step 1:   Instruct your child to write a story to correspond to pictures found in magazines.

Step 2:   Cut out the pictures and glue them to scraps of cardboard or poster board.

Step 3:   Stick a piece of magnetic tape to the back of each picture and use the back of a cookie sheet to display the pictures while the child tells the story (similar to a flannel board story).

As an alternative, have a child create a story by cutting out words from a magazine and gluing them to a single piece of construction paper. Because they can't always find the word they are looking for, the stories can turn out quite funny.

Straw Blowing

Materials needed:

Straws   Spoons
Poster paint   Saucers
Paper

Dip out a small amount of paint from a dish with a spoon. Place the drops of paint on the paper and let the children blow the drops through a straw. Tell them to blow lightly as they point the straw in different directions and watch the paint spread.

Feather Painting

Materials needed:

Large feathers
Poster paint
Paper

Have the children use feathers to paint as they would with a paintbrush. They can use either end of the feather to get different effects. When they are finished, wash the feathers out and let them dry.

Glass Wax Fun

Materials needed:

1 bottle glass wax (available with the cleaning aids in your grocery store)

Step 1:   Rub the wax all over a window and let it dry.

Step 2:   Let the children draw on the wax with their fingers, towels, or soft rags, creating their own designs. When the children are finished, wipe the window with a clean cloth and it will sparkle.

Puppets, Puppets, Puppets!

Materials needed:

Scrap paper
Paper lunch sacks
Glue
Markers
Popsicle sticks

Magazine
Large paper grocery sacks
Fabric scraps
Plastic spoons

Finger Puppets

Step 1: Copy each puppet on the following page onto stiff paper.

Step 2: Cut them out, and either staple or tape them together. Place each puppet over a finger and use them to help illustrate a story or just to play with.

Paper Stand-ups

Step 1: Fold a piece of heavy paper in half.

Step 2: Draw a picture on it, being sure that part of the picture touches the fold.

Step 3: Cut out the picture and stand it up.

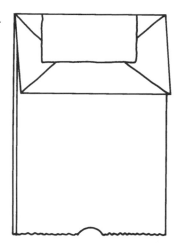

Sack Puppets

Step 1: Place a lunch sack on a table in front of you with the bottom of the sack facing you (as shown in the illustration at right).

Step 2: Draw a face and body on the sack with markers, or glue paper scraps to it to form the clothes, eyes, and other features. Be sure to situate the mouth where the edge of the sack bottom is folded against the sack.

Step 3: Put your hand inside of the sack and make the mouth move by moving your hand.

Hand Puppets

Step 1: Set your hand on top of both layers of a grocery sack and trace around it.

Step 2: Cut both layers out 1/4 inch away from the traced line and glue the edges together, leaving the bottom open for your hand to fit through. If there is writing on the sack, be sure to turn that side to the inside.

Step 3: Draw figures on the front and back of the hand puppet with markers. Add felt or fabric clothing if desired.

Stick Puppets

Step 1: Draw a picture on a piece of paper or cut one out of a magazine.

Step 2: If paper is very thin (like a magazine cutout), glue a stiffer piece of paper behind it to give it more strength.

Step 3: Glue a popsicle stick to the back of each one, and have fun!

Utensil Puppets

Step 1: Draw faces on plastic spoons with markers.

Step 2: Glue on clothes and hair made from fabric and yarn scraps.

2

Kids in the Kitchen

Kids in the Kitchen

I am often the first to shoo my children out of the kitchen when I am in a hurry to get a meal on the table. But children can actually help with a meal if you plan ahead. This chapter contains many ideas for fun edibles children can help with. For example, instead of preparing a cooked vegetable one evening, cut up several different veggies and let your children assemble them to make funny-looking animals. (They'll look darling on your plate and children have tons of fun making them. They *might* even eat the vegetables that they promised you they never would . . . "even when [they] grow up.")

Veggie Critters

Ingredients needed:

Zucchini   Radishes
Carrots   Pickles
Cucumbers   Green beans
Cauliflower   Bell pepper
Broccoli   Other raw vegetables
Olives   Toothpicks

Cut up as many different vegetables as you have into many different shapes. Be sure to have round shapes, square shapes, some long skinny shapes to use as legs, and some small pieces to use as eyes. The more shapes, the better.

Then, cut toothpicks into different sizes and let the children use them to attach one vegetable to another, as shown in the following diagram. One veggie critter per plate should be enough, but these are so fun to make, you may end up with enough for the entire week!

Homemade Ice-Cream Sandwiches

Ingredients needed:

Vanilla ice cream (brick form)
Hot fudge sauce
Peanut butter
Graham crackers

Break graham crackers in half (two rectangles per square). Cut ice cream into three-fourths-inch thick squares that are the same dimensions as the graham cracker squares. Spread a layer of peanut butter on one graham cracker square and a layer of hot fudge sauce on another square. Place a square of ice cream on the peanut butter and top it with the remaining graham cracker. Wrap each sandwich in plastic wrap and freeze until ready to eat.

Ice-Cream Clown

Ingredients needed:

Ice cream
Sugar cones
Colored candy-coated milk chocolate
candies, gum drops, maraschino
cherries, frosting, etc.
Sugar cookie (preferably with a scalloped
edge)

Set the cookie on a plate or in a dish. Scoop a ball of ice cream onto the cookie. Press the sugar cone on top of the ice cream ball to make the clown's hat. Using frosting and candies, make the clown's face and decorate his hat and cookie collar. Making this ice-cream clown is a fun activity in and of itself!

Fruit Kabobs

Ingredients needed:

Watermelon
Cantaloupe
Honeydew
Pineapple
Apples
Oranges
Peaches
Cherries
Other fruit
Bamboo skewers

Cut fruit into various shapes (cubes, balls, spears) and let the children help string them on the skewers. And, if you are barbecuing some evening, try barbecuing the fruit kabobs! That's right. Baste them with the following recipe and the fruit will be delicious, especially with ice cream.

Fruit glaze: Combine the following ingredients and baste over the barbecuing fruit: 1/4 cup honey, 1/2 cup orange juice, 1/2 cup lemon juice, 1 cup powdered sugar.

Funnel Fritters

Sometimes called squiggle bread, these delightful edibles can be seasoned with herbs, garlic, and cheese and served as an appetizer, or simply dusted with powdered sugar for a fun and wonderful dessert.

You can achieve various shapes and sizes by using different tools to drop the batter into hot vegetable oil. Although this is fun for the whole family to do, an adult should be present at all times (especially around the hot oil).

Ingredients needed:

1/2 cup butter
1 cup water
1 teaspoon sugar
1/4 teaspoon salt
1 cup all-purpose flour
4 eggs
Vegetable oil

Here's the basic recipe: In a two- or three-quart pan, melt butter over low heat. Add water, sugar, and salt. Turn the stove to high heat and bring mixture to a full boil. Add flour all at once, and stir until the batter becomes smooth, thick, and paste-like. As soon as the batter pulls away from the sides of the pan, remove the pan from the heat. Add the eggs one at a time, beating well after each one until the batter is smooth and shiny.

Heat oil to 400 degrees in a wok or deep frying pan. Drop or squeeze batter into the oil using a funnel, condiment squeeze bottle, cookie press, or pastry bag. Squeeze out a strand about four to eight inches long. Cut it off with a knife and squeeze out two or three more strands to cook at the same time. turn each strand over once. Total cooking time should be about five minutes. When done, lift fritters out of the oil with a slotted spoon and let them drain on paper towels.

For a dessert: Sprinkle cooked fritters with cinnamon and sugar or plain powdered sugar.

For an appetizer: Add the following to the water: 2 pressed cloves of garlic, 1 teaspoon dry basil, and 1/2 teaspoon dry thyme leaves. Then, after adding the eggs, stir 1/3 cup grated parmesan cheese into the batter.

Mother Goose Popcorn

This sweet, colorful popcorn has become a tradition for many families. For some reason, blue or green popcorn is more fun to eat.

Ingredients needed:

1 cup milk
1/2 cup butter
2 cups sugar
Food coloring
Approximately 1 1/2 cups popcorn
    kernels

Pop popcorn. In a saucepan, melt milk, butter, and sugar over medium heat. Bring mixture to a boil, stirring constantly, and cook until it reaches a soft ball stage (225 degrees). Remove from heat, add food coloring to make desired color, and mix well. Pour over popcorn, mixing until candy mixture thoroughly coats popcorn.

Cookie Cat Sundaes

Ingredients needed:

Favorite ice cream
Colored candy-coated milk chocolate candies
Small round cookies (chocolate or vanilla)
Red licorice vines
Small paper or plastic dishes

Place a big scoop of ice cream in each paper dish. This is the head for your Cookie Cat. Use candies for the eyes and mouth. For ears, push cookies into the top of the ice cream. For whiskers, stick several one-inch lengths of licorice into the ice cream on both sides of the nose. If you like, sprinkle on a little toasted coconut for hair. This is a fun variation to the run-of-the-mill sundae.

Chocolate Spiders

Ingredients needed:

1 eight-ounce milk-chocolate bar
2 cups crisp rice cereal
1/2 cup shredded coconut

Put the chocolate bar in a large microwave-safe bowl. Heat it in the microwave at low power for one minute, or slightly longer, until the chocolate melts. Stir in the cereal and coconut. Using a teaspoon, drop balls of the chocolate mixture onto waxed paper. Transfer the waxed paper and "spiders" to the refrigerator until the chocolate sets. Makes approximately 24 treats.

Ghost Suckers

Ingredients needed:

1 pound white chocolate (makes about twenty suckers)
Chocolate chips
Vegetable oil
Wooden popsicle sticks
Foil

Line a cookie sheet with foil. Spread vegetable oil on foil. Melt white chocolate in a double boiler pan, stirring frequently. As soon as the chocolate melts, drizzle ghost shapes onto the cookie sheet. Insert a wooden popsicle stick into each ghost. Before ghost sets, place two chocolate chips on for eyes. Refrigerate to help chocolate set. This is a great treat for Halloween!

Ice-Cream Cone Surprise

To turn an ordinary ice-cream cone into something fun for the kids—at the last minute—here is a simple, yet good, idea.

Ingredients needed:

Ice cream
Ice-cream cones
Candy

Place one or two candies (depending on their size) in the bottom of an ice-cream cone. Scoop on the ice cream as usual. When the kids get to the bottom they will find a fun surprise! Don't tell them that it is in there—just let them find it.

Chocolate Chimpanzees

Ingredients needed:

1 12-ounce package chocolate-flavored morsels
3 tablespoons vegetable oil
6 large, unpeeled bananas
24 almond slices
12 miniature marshmallows, split in half

Combine chocolate morsels with oil in the top of a double boiler pan. Place the pan over very hot tap water and let it stand, covered, for ten to fifteen minutes. Stir until chocolate chips are melted and the mixture is smooth. Slice bananas crosswise in half, then cut completely through skin (but not the banana) all the way around, about 1 1/2 inches from each end. Peel banana skin away from each end to where the skin was scored with the knife (see diagram).

For each banana, insert 2 almond slices on each side of the tip to look like ears. Dip the tip of the banana in chocolate, allowing chocolate to cover some of the peel. Allow chocolate to harden for several minutes.

Use a small paintbrush dipped in chocolate to "glue" marshmallow halves to the face for eyes. Dot marshmallows with chocolate for pupils, and stick two more marshmallow pieces onto the banana for the mouth. Freeze.

Watermelon Sherbet

Ingredients needed:

1/2 gallon lime sherbet
1/2 gallon pineapple sherbet
1 gallon raspberry sherbet
Semi-sweet chocolate chips

Put a very large mixing bowl (or two medium-sized mixing bowls) in the freezer until cold. Leave the lime sherbet out of the freezer until it is slightly soft and spreadable. Using a large spoon, spread a thin layer (one-quarter inch) of lime sherbet onto the inside of the bowl, all the way to the rim. Put the bowl in the freezer until the sherbet hardens, and take the pineapple sherbet out of the freezer to soften.

When the lime sherbet has hardened, take it out of the freezer and spread a slightly thicker layer of pineapple sherbet on top of the lime sherbet. Put it in the freezer to harden, and set out the raspberry sherbet to soften. When the pineapple sherbet has hardened, fill the rest of the bowl with the softened raspberry sherbet. Freeze.

When ready to serve, set the bowl in a sink filled with hot water (be careful not to let any water go over the brim of your bowl). When the sherbet loosens from the side of the bowl, turn it upside down and slice it as you would a watermelon. Place each slice on individual plates and push several chocolate chips into each one to look like watermelon seeds.

This is as much fun to serve as it is to eat!

3

"This Is the
Night We've
Waited For"

(Family Home Evening Group Ideas)

"This Is the Night We've Waited For"
(Family Home Evening Group Ideas)

Soon after the birth of my first child, Amanda, my husband and I began to think more seriously about what we could do to have meaningful family home evenings in our home. It started with just devoting Monday evening to being with each other—no meetings, no outside commitments. We would watch a movie, play a game, or just read. Usually Amanda would sleep through the whole evening—but, we started a tradition.

Then, as daughter number two came, and Amanda was old enough to sing a song and listen to a story, we began a more structured program—a very *short* structured program. As my husband and I became busier and busier, it became increasingly difficult to plan ahead. Does this sound familiar?

"Great dinner, honey. Now, what's planned for family night?" says Dad.

"Is tonight Monday already? You do the dishes. I'll figure out something real quick," Mom says.

About the same time that I was feeling very inadequate in the family home evening department, we moved into a new ward and my visiting teacher invited me to be a part of her *Family Home Evening Group.* I had never heard of such a group but went to a meeting anyway. She assured me that this would make planning and holding family home evenings easier. She was right.

This chapter is full of ideas for you to start your own group—there are many ways to do it, and I'll show you a few. Basically, the idea behind all of these groups is to find several friends who have children of similar ages. Once a month (usually), all of the women will get together and exchange their ideas. Some groups will simply exchange ideas, and others will exchange finished products: flannel board stories, refrigerator magnets, and object lessons, to name a few.

Choose the group idea that is best for you and your friends, or make up one of your own! Whatever you do, do it.

If you will take time to organize a set of files by topic for the family home evening stories that you will acquire, your children will never be without a talk in Primary!

Group 1

Step 1:   Decide as a group which day of the month to meet and at what time of day. (This can be the most difficult task of all.)

Step 2:   Decide which topics you want to cover during the year (one per month).

Step 3:   Decide what types of things you want the group to prepare each month (such as flannel board stories, scriptures, music, and object lessons).

Step 4:   Fill out a six-month chart containing all of this information, as well as every member's name and phone number, and make a copy for everyone. (A ready-to-use chart that you can cut out and copy is found on p. 33; a completed sample chart is found on p. 31.) Every six months you will assess the group's needs and fill out another six-month chart.

Each member of this group will bring eight fully completed items of the type they were assigned. On the following chart, you will see that in March, Jane Jones will bring eight packets, each containing one scripture story on faith and a visual aid to go with it. She will also exchange each packet for things that the other seven women will bring.

The group will meet at Betty Boop's house (the hostess), who will provide the refreshments—a fun recipe for family home evening. A recipe card also should be sent home with each member so they will be able to use Betty's idea during the month.

Sample

Family Home Evening Group						
6 Months:	January 1st	February 5th	March 5th	April 2nd	May 7th	June 4th
Topics:	Goals	Freedom of Choice	Faith	Gossip	Prophets	Love
Sue Smith 555-1212	1	2	3	4	5	6
Cathy Carr 555-1219	2	3	4	5	6	7
Polly Pace 555-1218	3	4	5	6	7	8
Dawn Davis 555-1217	4	5	6	7	8	1
Mary Moore 555-1216	5	6	7	8	1	2
Betty Boop 555-1215	6	7	8	1	2	3
Ann Anders 555-1214	7	8	1	2	3	4
Jane Jones 555-1213	8	1	2	3	4	5

Assignments

1 — Flannel board story
2 — Scripture story (with visual aid)
3 — Fun story or object lesson (with visual aid)
4 — Activity or craft

5 — Scripture (to display during the month)
6 — Music (with visual aid)
7 — Miscellaneous
8 — Hostess

Family Home Evening Group						
6 Months:						
Topics:						
	1	2	3	4	5	6
	2	3	4	5	6	7
	3	4	5	6	7	8
	4	5	6	7	8	1
	5	6	7	8	1	2
	6	7	8	1	2	3
	7	8	1	2	3	4
	8	1	2	3	4	5

Assignments

1 — Flannel board story
2 — Scripture story (with visual aid)
3 — Fun story or object lesson
      (with visual aid)
4 — Activity or craft

5 — Scripture (to display during
      the month)
6 — Music (with visual aid)
7 — Miscellaneous
8 — Hostess

Group 2

This idea is great for four or five people who (1) have small children and get the *Friend* magazine or have older children and get the *New Era*, (2) have a copy of the Church *Family Home Evening Resource Book*, (3) have a *Children's Songbook* and the hymnbook, and (4) have a set of scriptures.

Step 1: Decide on which day of the month you want to meet.

Step 2: Decide which topics you want to cover each month.

Step 3: Fill out a six-month assignment chart for everyone to take home, including everyone's name and phone number. (A ready-to-use chart that you can cut out and copy is found on p. 37; a completed sample chart is found on p. 36.)

Every member of this group will bring a three-by-five-inch card for everyone, with all of the resource information needed to hold a fun family night. The resources should include only those listed above, so everyone will be able to easily find every item listed. This card should include an opening song, a scripture-based story, a fictional story, an activity idea, a scripture, and a fun recipe. (A completed sample is found on p. 39.)

If a member of the group finds a great story that she wants to share, but it is not in one of the resources listed above, she should make a copy of the story for everyone to take home, provided the story is not in copyright. (Bear in mind that generally a copyrighted story cannot legally be copied without permission.)

The sample chart on the next page shows that in February, the group will meet at Doris Night's home. All will go prepared to exchange their three-by-five-inch cards filled with easily accessible stories, activities, and songs. Since many of the stories will be coming out of the Church magazines, it isn't necessary to prepare visual aids—the pictures have already been drawn.

This organization works best if each member of the group has at least a couple of years' worth of Church magazines filed away.

Sample

Family Home Evening Group			
DATE	TIME	TOPIC	HOSTESS
January 1st	8:00 p.m.	Priesthood	Barbara Shrub 555-1212
February 5th	8:00 p.m.	Service	Doris Night 555-1213
March 5th	8:00 p.m.	Tithing	Annie Sprucely 555-1214
April 3rd	8:00 p.m.	Manners	Debbie Saran 555-1215
May 7th	8:00 p.m.	Obedience	Barbara Shrub 555-1212
June 4th	8:00 p.m.	Pioneers	Doris Night 555-1213

Family Home Evening Group			
DATE	TIME	TOPIC	HOSTESS

Sample

3 x 5 Card — Side 1

	Faith
Opening Song:	"I Know My Father Lives," (*Children's Song-book*, pg. 5).
Scripture Story:	Story of the people of Anti-Nephi-Lehi who buried their weapons, having faith that their sins would be forgiven them if they took no more blood (Book of Mormon, Alma 24).
Fictional Story:	"Coal Pitts," (*Friend*, Aug. 1990, pg. 27).

3 x 5 Card — Side 2

Activity:	Play a variation of "Blind Man's Bluff." Set up an obstacle course in your home. Let everyone have a turn to be blindfolded and exercise his/her faith in trusting the rest of the family to give correct directions through the maze.
Scripture:	Scriptures are answered according to our faith (Mosiah 27:14).
Fun Recipe:	Banana Bug (*Friend*, July 1990, pg.18).

Group 3

The following organization is great for eight to ten people who want stories *only* and plan to meet every other month.

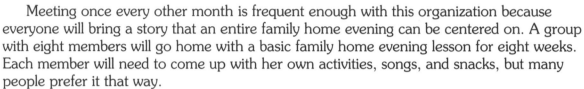

Step 1: Decide when you want to meet.

Step 2: Decide which topics you will follow.

Step 3: Fill out a reminder chart for *everyone* to keep at home. (A ready-to-use chart that you can cut out and copy is found on p. 43; a completed sample chart is found on p. 41.)

Meeting once *every* other month is frequent enough with this organization because everyone will bring a story that an entire family home evening can be centered on. A group with eight members will go home with a basic family home evening lesson for eight weeks. Each member will need to come up with her own activities, songs, and snacks, but many people prefer it that way.

According to the accompanying sample chart, on January 1, Debbie Richardson will be responsible for bringing a true story (contemporary) to share with each member of the group. The group will meet at Gaye Jones's house that night.

Sample

Family Home Evening Group						
12 Month Calendar:	January 1st	March 5th	May 7th	July 6th	September 4th	November 3rd
Topics:	Account-ability	Self-Esteem	Baptism	Sacrament	Fasting	Thankful-ness
Diane Middents 555-1111	1	2	3	4	5	1
Carole Jones 555-2222	2	3	4	5	1	2
Mary Egbert 555-3333	3	4	5	1	2	3
Debbie Richardson 555-4444	4	5	1	2	3	4
Diana Tanner 555-5555	2	1	2	3	4	5
Polly Crum 555-6666	1	2	3	4	3	1
Gaye Jones 555-7777	5	3	4	2	1	2
Kay Ferrin 555-8888	3	4	2	1	2	3

Assignments

1 — Flannel board story
2 — Fictional story

3 — Scripture story
4 — True story (contemporary)

5 — Hostess

Family Home Evening Group						
12 Month Calendar:						
Topics:						
	1	2	3	4	5	1
	2	3	4	5	1	2
	3	4	5	1	2	3
	4	5	1	2	3	4
	2	1	2	3	4	5
	1	2	3	4	3	1
	5	3	4	2	1	2
	3	4	2	1	2	3

Assignments

1 — Flannel board story   3 — Scripture story
2 — Fictional story   4 — True story (contemporary)

5 — Hostess

Group 4

This organization is designed for either six or twelve members and takes a great effort once or twice a year, depending on how many are in the group. If the group has six people, it will meet twice a year. If the group has twelve, it will meet once a year.

Step 1: Decide on a date to exchange materials (about one month away).

Step 2: Decide which topics will be covered. Each member will be assigned one topic for one month and will provide something from every category listed on the chart for every member of the group.

Step 3: Fill out a reminder chart for everyone to take home. (A ready-to-use chart that you can cut out and copy is found on p. 47; a completed sample chart is found on p. 46.)

This may seem like a lot of work, especially if you choose to have twelve in your group. However, you will find that as you search for one particular item (a flannel board story, for example), you will also run across scripture stories, fictional stories, and other useful material. As a result, finding the material will not be difficult or time-consuming. What *will* take time is coloring and cutting out six or twelve flannel board stories and any visual aids that go with the other stories you have chosen. Once the work is done, however, you are finished for six months or maybe even a year!

Sample

Family Home Evening Group Exchange Date: June 23rd, 8:00 p.m., Monica's house	
Cathy Ostergar 555-9999	"Love Thy Neighbor"
Monica Markoff 555-0000	"Christmas"
Virginia Bird 555-1111	"Thanksgiving"
Jessie Pitcher 555-2222	"Pioneer Day"
Milena Delgado 555-333	"Do What is Right"
Marian Killian 555-4444	"Prophets"

Assignments

Everyone is to provide one of each item listed below for *every* member of the group.

— Flannel board story
— Fictional story
— Scripture story
— True story
— Activity or craft
— Song suggestion (with visual aid)
— Fun recipe idea

Family Home Evening Group Exchange Date:	

Assignments

Everyone is to provide one of each item listed below for every member of the group.

— Flannel board story
— Fictional story
— Scripture story
— True story
— Activity or craft
— Song suggestion (with visual aid)
— Fun recipe idea

General Family Home Evening
Organizational Tips

If you prefer organizing your family home evenings on your own, here are some suggestions to make it easier:

1. File all Church magazines and keep them in an easily accessible spot. The December issues are crucial—they include an index of everything that was in every issue of the preceding year.

2. Become familiar with the Church *Family Home Evening Resource Book*. There is a lot of great information, suggestions, and stories that have been written for all ages.

3. Dedicate a couple of hours each month to the planning, copying, coloring, cutting out, and laminating of family home evening materials, stories, and visual aids. Get your children involved! They will love to help you color and cut things out. If your children are older, give them assignments to dig through the family home evening manual and Church magazines to find stories they would enjoy learning and sharing with the family.

4. Take advantage of your ward's library. There are many wonderful resources in there to help you with your family home evenings. Some examples are:

   — Video tapes on a wide array of topics (families are forever, missionary work, kindness, and so forth).

   — Flannel board stories (not available in all libraries).

   — Church magazines. If you do not get the Church magazines or are just starting your family and have a limited library, take advantage of your ward's collection.

4

Family Fun Ideas

Family Fun Ideas

An activity can be a great way of teaching an important lesson to children (and adults) in a way that will be remembered for a long time. In this chapter I am going to share with you some of my favorite family activities and service projects that your family will have as much fun planning as they will doing.

Activities

Mama's Café

This activity will teach your young children the value of a dollar.

Step 1:   Turn your kitchen into a restaurant by decorating the table with a special tablecloth and centerpiece. Set up a hostess stand where your children must wait to be seated. If possible, tack up a sheet or two to the ceiling to block the kitchen from the table's view (or you may just want to seat them in your dining room or set the table outside if weather permits).

Step 2:   Create menus with your children's favorite foods, such as peanut butter and jelly sandwiches, hamburgers, hot dogs, macaroni and cheese, chocolate milk, punch, chips, and french fries. (The following page contains a sample menu. A ready-to-use menu that you can cut out and copy is found on p. 55.)

Step 3:   Give out play money from a board game or copy the sample money on p. 57.

Step 4:   Plan some type of entertainment. If you have musical ability, play and/or sing to your guests. If not, lip-sync your children's favorite music. Use your imagination.

Step 5:   Soup's on! Seat your children. Explain that they will be given X dollars to spend, and should spend wisely. If they spend it all on junk food and are hungry later, the kitchen will be closed. If they *overspend*, they will have to do the dishes to make up for the money they are short. Have fun!

Sample

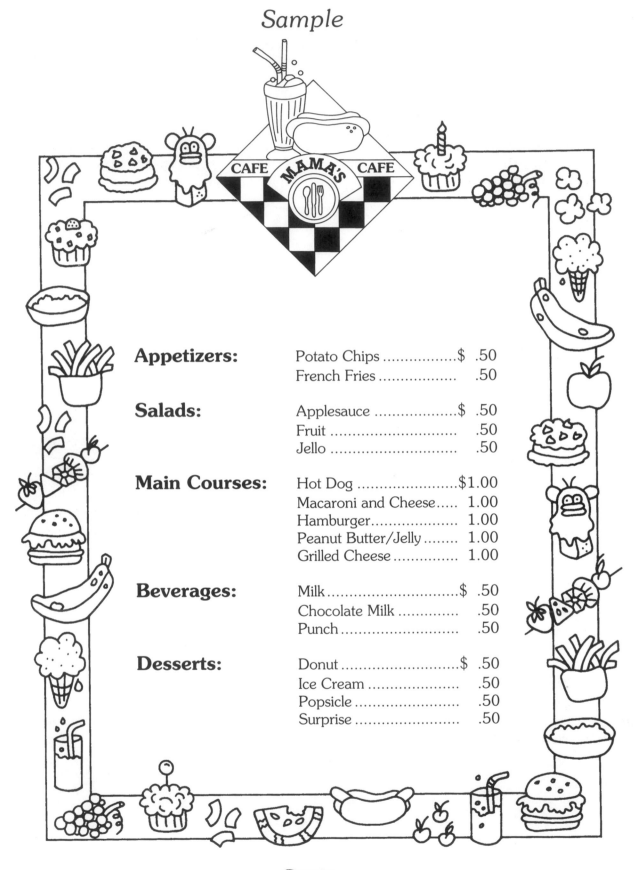

Appetizers: Potato Chips ....$ .50
                   French Fries 50

Salads: Applesauce ....$ .50
                   Fruit 50
                   Jello 50

Main Courses: Hot Dog $1.00
                   Macaroni and Cheese..... 1.00
                   Hamburger................... 1.00
                   Peanut Butter/Jelly 1.00
                   Grilled Cheese 1.00

Beverages: Milk............................$ .50
                   Chocolate Milk 50
                   Punch 50

Desserts: Donut ....$ .50
                   Ice Cream 50
                   Popsicle 50
                   Surprise 50

Appetizers:

Salads:

Main Courses:

Beverages:

Desserts:

Family/Neighborhood Olympics

This activity will teach your children sportsmanship.

Step 1: Plan and prepare the games you want to play.

Step 2: Make awards (ready-to-use awards that you can cut out and copy are found on p. 61 and p. 63).

Step 3: Plan menu for backyard barbecue.

Step 4: Make and send out invitations to family and/or friends. (Materials for making the invitations are found on found on p. 63 and p. 65.)

Step 5: Try to obtain the official Olympic music and play it during the opening ceremonies. Also, find your national anthem to play during the awards ceremonies at the end.

Step 6: Buy a backyard tiki torch (from an import store) to use during the opening ceremonies. Have someone run into your backyard carrying the lighted torch. Then, to officially open the games, have them light the barbecue with the tiki torch (be sure there is plenty of lighter fluid on the coals). If you do not have a barbecue, light another tiki torch in place of it.

Step 7: Let the games begin! Play the games, record the scores, and have an awards ceremony afterwards. Set up three platforms, the middle one being slightly higher, for the three top winners to stand on. All other participants should receive participation awards and be recognized as well.

Step 8: Have a party!

Game Ideas

Slam dunk contest: If you have a basketball standard at your house, this can be a really funny competition. Rate the dunks on originality, level of difficulty, and execution.

Slip 'n slide contest: This contest works best in the summertime, of course, but if you have some adventurous participants, it can be really funny in cold weather. Set up a large plastic tarp on the lawn and turn on the hose or the sprinklers. Have participants run and slide on the plastic. Rate slides on originality, level of difficulty, length of ride, and execution.

Wheelbarrow race: This is an old standby, one that people of all ages can play and enjoy. In case you have forgotten how, one person puts his/her hands on the ground while his partner grabs the first person's feet, lifts them up, and "rolls" him like a wheelbarrow across the finish line. The first team to cross the finish line wins.

One-legged long jump: If you have a sandbox at home that sits flush with the ground, use it for the participants to jump into. If not, simply spray-paint or tape a starting line on your grass and mark the distance of your participant's jumps (one-legged, of course) on the grass with their names written on pieces of tape. The one who jumps the farthest is the winner.

No-smile contest: This one is fun to do. Two people stare at each other until one smiles. Making faces at each other to elicit a smile is okay as long as the faces do not include a smile (the judges will have to closely monitor this one). Start with two contestants; the winner stays, and another challenger tries to beat him. This contest only has a first-place winner, but it is lots of fun to video tape.

You may copy and use the awards as they appear here, or you can cut off the ribbon part of the illustration and glue 10-inch lengths of blue, red, white, and purple ribbon to the back of the round section. The awards look nice when copied on yellow cardstock.

Copy, cut out, and fill in party information. Glue information to the invitation found on p. 65 .

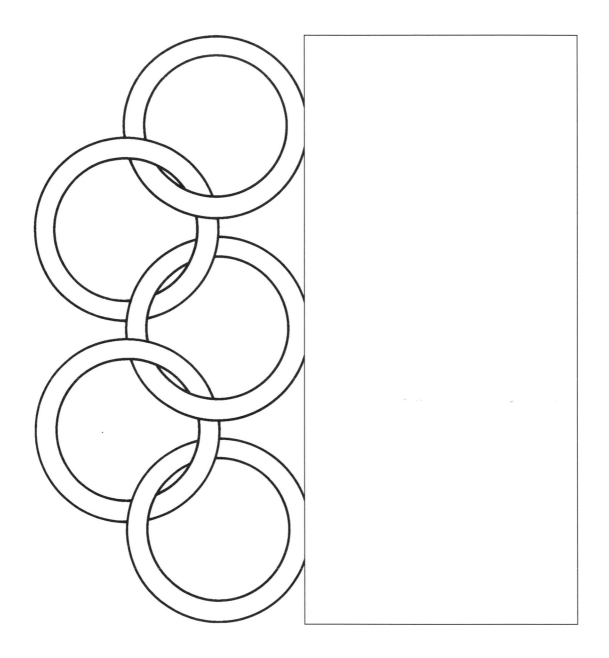

Copy, cut out, and glue the party information from p. 63 to the rectangular half of the invitation underneath the Olympic rings (use rubber cement or spray adhesive).

Home Theater

Although this activity takes some organization and will help your children learn how to plan an activity, it is mostly done just for the fun of it.

Step 1: Make a marquee and hang it over or near your front door.

Step 2: Rent or borrow a big screen television if possible (it is not necessary).

Step 3: Copy tickets and invitations and send them at least one week in advance to the families you want to invite. (Ready-to-use tickets and invitations that you can copy and cut out are found on p. 69.)

Step 4: Copy snack coupons to hand out at the door to your guests. (Ready-to-use coupons that you can copy and cut out are found on p. 69.)

Step 5: Rent a movie that will be appropriate for all ages.

Step 6: Make and buy items for a snack bar and set up a table for it.

Step 7: Set up chairs and/or pillows for all guests to sit on.

Step 8: When the guests arrive, give them coupons to use at the snack bar for popcorn, pop, candy, or whatever else you would like to include.

Step 9: Have fun!

You're Invited

What: _____

Where: _____

Date: _____

Time: _____

(Remember to bring your tickets)

TICKET Admit One   **TICKET** Admit One   **TICKET** Admit One   **TICKET** Admit One

TICKET Admit One   **TICKET** Admit One   **TICKET** Admit One   **TICKET** Admit One

---

COUPON Exchange for 1 Snack   **COUPON** Exchange for 1 Snack   **COUPON** Exchange for 1 Snack   **COUPON** Exchange for 1 Snack

COUPON Exchange for 1 Snack   **COUPON** Exchange for 1 Snack   **COUPON** Exchange for 1 Snack   **COUPON** Exchange for 1 Snack

Personal Songs

It has been a tradition in my family for many generations to write a special song for each member of the family as they are born or married into the group. You don't have to have any particular musical talent to do this and it will give your children a real sense of individual worth and importance.

Step 1: Choose a familiar song that has an easy melody to remember. If you are writing a song for a newborn, choose a melody you like. If you are writing it for an older child, choose one of their favorite songs.

Step 2: Rewrite the words to the tune you chose, describing your child and why they are so special. If this is a problem for you, try using many of the same words, and just change a few here and there to make it more personal. For example, my daughter Rebecca's song is to the tune *You Are My Sunshine*. The first line of that song reads:

"You are my sunshine, my only sunshine . . . "

Rebecca's song begins:

"Rebecca, darling, you bring us sunshine . . . "

This needn't be a difficult or time-consuming project. Some of my family's favorite songs to sing are the ones that took only a few minutes to write. Here are a couple of examples:

Deborah's Song
to the tune of *Pretty Baby*

Everybody loves our Deborah,
That's why we're in love with you.
Little Deborah, our sweet Deborah.
With eyes so bright you're pure delight
Your bring us so much joy.
Little Deborah, our sweet Deborah.
Your winsome smile, we love it,
And all your winning ways
You have stolen all our hearts.
Boom! Boom!
Everybody loves our Deborah,
That's why we're in love with you.
(Ba, da, da, da!)
Little Deborah of ours,
I mean to tell ya.'
(Ba, da, da, da!)
Little Deborah ours!

Amanda's Song
to the tune of *Singin' in the Rain*

Amanda Panda Bear, Amanda Panda Bear,
With that smile on your face,
And your golden brown hair.

You love to play, you're a little bit shy.
You brighten our day
With that gleam in your eye.

Angels cried a tear when you came to the earth.
They would miss you so much,
But rejoiced at your birth.

We're happy you're here
Life is grand when you're near.
Amanda, we love you dear!

These special songs are sung at birthdays, whenever one of the children is spotlighted in Primary, and every other time we can find an excuse. They claim to be embarrassed, but we know that they love it. I did—and still do!

Family Movie

This will take several weeks to complete. Although it may seem that your older children (teenagers) feel silly acting out a play, you might be surprised how involved they become once you get started.

Week 1: Plan the script. Try acting out a Bible or Book of Mormon story or reenacting a funny family experience (such as a vacation). Children's books are also excellent sources for scripts. Have a narrator and assign various speaking parts for characters who are speaking in the story. Put each person in charge of making their own costume. Younger children may need some help from older siblings or Mom and Dad.

Week 2: Shoot the movie with a home video camera. Some tips on shooting a good video are:

1. Use a tripod whenever possible.

2. Film indoors at night or outdoors during the day.

3. Once you think you have plenty of light to shoot a good video, add two or three more light sources.

4. Use all of the microphone equipment you can get your hands on; there's nothing worse than going to all that work and not being able to hear the dialogue.

5. Goofs and mistakes are fine; in fact, they will be more fun to watch later.

Week 3: Watch the movie, complete with popcorn. Invite grandparents if possible and give them a copy (or send it in the mail).

Backyard Waterpark

You don't need to have a pool in your backyard to have tons of fun in the heat of the summer. Here are some suggestions:

1. Set a plastic baby pool at the bottom of your swing set slide. Run a hose up to the top and you have a water slide!

2. Set up several slip 'n' slides or one large plastic tarp on the lawn. Turn on the sprinklers and let children either run through the sprinklers or slip on the plastic.

3. Set up a squirt gun table. Let children fill squirt guns in buckets of water.

4. Set up a table with bubble-blowing equipment—plastic strawberry baskets, which make hundreds of bubbles at once, pieces of PVC pipe, coat hangers bent into different shapes, and even small hula hoops all work great! Start by making your own bubble solution: 1 quart water, 1 cup dishwashing liquid, 2 tablespoons glycerin. (To use a hula hoop you will need to make several batches of bubble solution to fill two or three inches of a small plastic baby pool. Set the hula hoop inside and have a child stand in the middle of the hoop. Slowly pull the hoop over the child's head to completely surround the child with the bubble—this is lots of fun!)

5. Set up a Popsicle stand.

6. Set aside one area where kids (and adults) can go to get dry if they wish—and have plenty of towels!

Service Projects

A service project is a wonderful way to teach and learn about the really important things in life. Serving others give us a warm, good feeling that remains for a long time. Here are a few suggestions for your family to try:

1. Pick up trash around your ward's meetinghouse.

2. Do yard work for a neighbor in need.

3. Make a card and bake something for someone who needs some extra caring.

4. Be pixies for a week. Draw names so each member of the family is in charge of doing special, secret things for another member.

5. Take a housewarming gift to a new family in your neighborhood.

6. Participate in a "Sub-for-Santa" program during Christmastime. Try making special gifts like wreaths, dolls, food, or Christmas tree ornaments. Take extra care to be sensitive to the needs and feelings of the person or family you will be sponsoring. Do it out of love, not pity.

7. Hold your own Deseret Industries drive. Call friends and family for donations and bring the items to the DI or give them to a specific family.

8. Prepare a program for a nursing home—some time *other* than Christmas. Plan musical numbers or a puppet show. If your family has older children, a variety show complete with a comedian would be fun.

9. Prepare a puppet show for the children's ward of a local hospital—and leave the puppets there for the children to enjoy later.

Last-Minute Activity Ideas

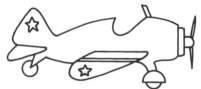

1. Visit the airport and watch the planes take off and land.

2. Go to the mountains and gather firewood (if legal in your area).

3. Visit a museum.

4. Have a picnic and feed the ducks.

5. Go to the zoo.

6. Go on a nature hunt. Divide into teams and see who can bring back the greatest number of different types of leaves, flowers, rocks, and other items.

7. Make Christmas cards.

8. Have an impromptu talent show.

9. Have a family slumber party—watch a movie, pop popcorn, and sleep together in the same room in sleeping bags.

10. Ride bikes.

11. Pretend to have an emergency such as a fire, a medical emergency, or a stranger at the door with Mom and Dad away. Act out the correct things to do for different emergency situations.

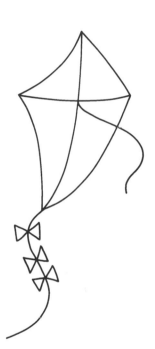

12. Make surprise ice cream. Go to the store and give everyone one dollar to buy something to put into the vanilla ice cream as it is churning. As long as nobody brings home string beans, the ice cream *usually* turns out great!

13. Roast marshmallows.

14. Pull taffy.

15. Eat dinner backwards (dessert first and appetizers last).

16. Make and fly kites at the park.

17. Have a "Who Knows Whom Best" night. Give everyone twenty questions to answer about different family members, such as favorite color, where were they born, favorite animal, and so forth. Then see who knows whom best.

18. Bring dinner to Dad's office and take a tour.

19. Have a hopscotch tournament.

20. Make bird feeders by stringing bread, seeds, nuts, or popcorn onto a string, several inches apart, and attaching each end of the string to a tree trunk or branch.

Birthday Party—for Your House!

Once a year (the anniversary of the day you moved in) give your home a thorough, top-to-bottom, inside-and-out cleaning. Plan a big party for the family when the work is done, and give the house a present. Here are some suggestions (see following pages for detailed instructions).

Southwest Coffee Table: Simply lash sticks together and set a piece of glass on top. (This is a great activity for the Scouts in the family to help with.)

Checkerboard Area Rug: Made with carpet scraps, this is an inexpensive and decorative rug that will be fun for the family to use for years to come. You can even use it as a giant game board.

Paint a Room or Two: Everyone can help spruce up a less-than-lively room in your home by using paint and sponges, rags, or plastic wrap.

PVC Pipe Table: With just a few tools you can make a sturdy table for your children for about twenty-five dollars.

Children's Folk Art: Transfer your children's artwork onto wood, cut out the shape, and make a stand. It will look great on any bookshelf, and your house will love it.

Southwest Coffee Table

Materials needed:

24 to 32 branches that measure about 1 1/2 inches in diameter
Paint wash (use one part oil base paint to one part paint thinner)
Twine or leather laces
Tempered glass, at least 1/2-inch thick, with sanded edges

Step 1: Trim branches to desired length. For a thirty-eight-inch square table, cut branches thirty-six-inches long (the glass tabletop will extend one inch beyond the branches on all four sides).

Step 2: Apply wash by wiping paint on with a rag and wiping it off again with a clean rag. Some paint will remain giving branches a washed look. Let dry.

Step 3: Using twine or leather laces, lash branches together starting and ending with the straightest branches. The accompanying illustration shows instructions for lashing.

Step 4: Place glass on top of branches and make sure it is level. If it is not, shim it up wherever necessary.

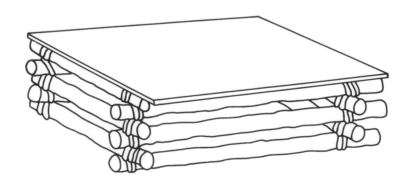

Lashing Instructions: (also found in the *Official Boy Scout Handbook*)

Twist rope end around standing part

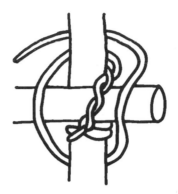

First wrapping

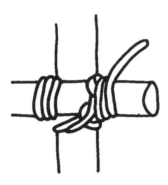

Third wrapping

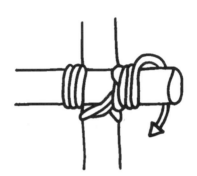

Ready for frapping

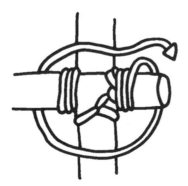

Frapping

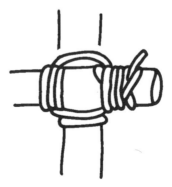

Square lashing complete

Checkerboard Area Rug

Materials needed:

1 large, bound carpet sample the size you want your finished rug to be (a typical size
    is 27-by-48-inches)
Miscellaneous carpet scraps in various colors
1 piece of denim, canvas, or other sturdy fabric at least the same size as large, bound
    carpet sample
Carpet adhesive
Small trowel
Utility knife with plenty of spare blades
Poster board
Wide tape
4 1/3 yards of grosgrain ribbon
Hot glue

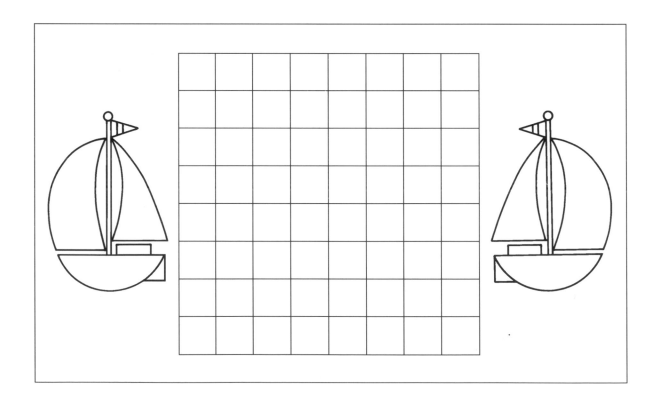

Step 1: Draw your checkerboard pattern. The center of the finished rug will be the checkerboard, and working with a 27-by-16-inch carpet, the checkerboard will measure 24-by-24 inches (64, 3-inch squares). Draw this checkerboard onto the back of the carpet.

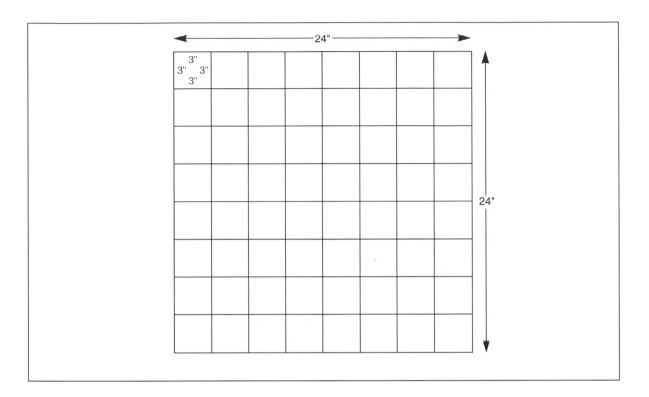

Step 2: Now, draw a simple design on the poster board to match your child's bedroom, such as a flower or boat design from the wallpaper (simple ABCs and 123s are cute, too). Remember, it needs to fit into the space remaining on either side of the checkerboard (it will measure about 27-by-12 inches). Cut *outline* of the design out of the poster board and trace its outline onto the back of the carpet.

Step 3: Using a utility knife, cut out the outlines you have drawn on the back of the carpet. *Note:* If one of the colors you are using in your checkerboard is the same as the large carpet sample you are working with, do not cut the outer squares of the checkerboard that will be that color. However, you will need to cut 18 squares of that color to glue into the middle.

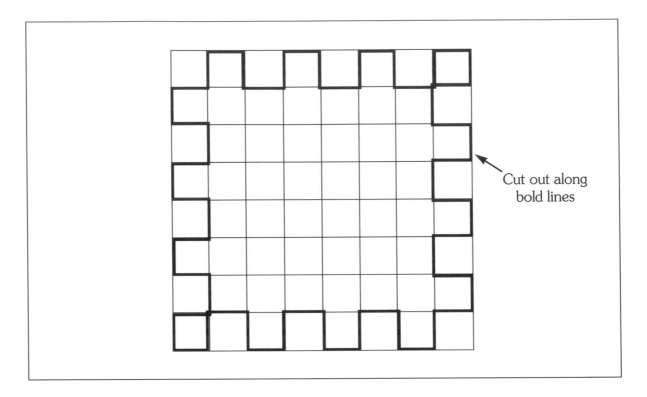

Cut out along bold lines

Step 4: Cut 32, 3-inch squares out of contrasting carpet color for the checkerboard.

Step 5: Cut your "design" pattern into separate pattern pieces for the different colors you want to use. Transfer these patterns onto the backs of carpet scraps and cut them out. If you have a lot of similar pieces, it may be necessary to number them to be sure they get put into the right place on your rug.

Step 6: Tape the canvas to a large flat surface (a garage floor, for example). Following directions on the can, apply adhesive to the back of the large, bound carpet sample. Place it on top of the canvas.

Step 7: Apply adhesive to all carpet pieces one at a time, and put rug together like a puzzle.

Step 8: Turn the rug over, cut off the excess canvas, and hot glue grosgrain ribbon to cover the raw edge of the canvas. The rug is finished! Now use it as a giant game board if you want to!

Suggestions for playing pieces:

Two different colors of blocks
Round crackers (just be sure to vacuum after the game)
Canning lids decorated with two different colors of paint or wallpaper scraps
Thin wooden cutouts from a craft store, painted two different ways
Traditional playing pieces from a board game you already have

Paint a Room or Two

Sponge Painting

Materials needed:

Sponges (just about any kind will work, but I like the look a big natural sea sponge
    gives best)
Paint (oil-based washes work well, but you can use any type of paint; different paints
    will give you different looks)
Turpentine or mineral spirits (use to thin oil-based paints)
Water (use to thin water-based paints)

Sponge Painting Instructions

Step 1: Saturate sponge with watered-down or thinned paint and squeeze out the excess.

Step 2: Dab the sponge onto the wall until the paint is thin enough to see through. Repeat until the wall is finished.

Step 3: If desired, sponge another complementing color over the first. Leave some of the bare wall showing through and try to use lighter colors. Dark colors can be *too much*, especially if two or more are used on the same wall.

Sponge Painting Instructions (Variation)

Step 1: Paint a 3-by-3-foot area of your wall with the color of paint you have chosen.

Step 2: Using a damp sponge (dampened with either turpentine or water), dab wet paint off the wall. Press firmly and try rolling the sponge up the wall. Repeat.

Rag Painting

Materials needed:

Old cotton rags (cloth diapers work great)
Paint of your choice
Mineral spirits or turpentine (use to thin oil-based paints)
Water (use to thin water-based paints)

Rag Painting Instructions

Step 1: Saturate a small piece of rag (approximately one square foot) with thinned paint and wring out the excess.

Step 2: Scrunch up the rag and roll it up the wall, pressing firmly.

Step 3: Repeat until the wall is finished. When paint is dry, you may want to rag on another color over it for a different effect.

Rag Painting Instructions (Variation)

Step 1: Paint a 3-by-3-foot section of wall with the color of paint you have chosen.

Step 2: Scrunch up the rag and roll it up the wall, removing some of the paint you just applied.

Step 3: Repeat the process, working on small sections of wall at a time so the paint doesn't dry before you can rag it off.

Plastic Wrap Painting

Materials needed:

Plastic wrap
Paint (any kind)
Paint roller
Big tarp for the floor

Plastic Wrap Painting Instructions

Step 1: Tear off a 2½-to-3-foot-long piece of plastic wrap. Set it down on a plastic tarp and paint it, using a paint roller.

Step 2: Carefully lift up the plastic wrap and press the painted side onto the wall.

Step 3: Peel off the plastic wrap.

Step 4: Repeat the process, using the same piece of plastic wrap as long as it works well.

Plastic Wrap Painting Instructions (Variation)

Step 1: Paint small sections of the wall at a time.

Step 2: Press clean pieces of plastic wrap onto the wall and them peel them off, removing some paint and leaving an interesting pattern as well.

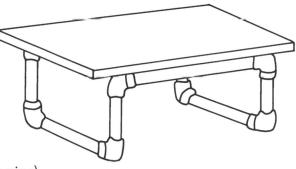

PVC Pipe Table

Materials needed:

12 feet of 1 1/2-inch-diameter PVC
    pipe
8 elbows, 90 degrees (to fit 1 1/2 inch pipe)
1 sink cutout, about 22-by-31 inches (contract a cabinetmaker for this; for a small
    price he will also round off the corners and band the edges with plastic laminate)
4 round-head screws, 2 1/2 inches long and 10-pound weight
PVC cement
Lacquer thinner
Tools: pencil, measuring tape, fine-toothed saw or tube cutter, knife, drill, 3/16-inch
    bit, screwdriver, and fine sandpaper

Step 1: Measure and cut the pipe into the following dimensions:
  (A) Two 22-inch pieces
  (B) Four 18-inch pieces
  (C) Two 14-inch pieces

Step 2: Clean the black writing off of the pipe with lacquer thinner and roughen the ends of the pipe with sandpaper.

Step 3: Drill 3/16-inch holes through (A) pieces for the screws that attach to the top (see diagram).

Step 4: Cement the pieces together, following the diagram.

Step 5: Place the tabletop on the table. Use a pencil to mark the underneath side where the screws will drill into the top. Punch a small hole in each mark (this will make it easier to drill into the tabletop).

Step 6: Drill from the underside of the pipe up into the tabletop. Before screwing the screws into the tabletop, check to be sure that they are not too long.

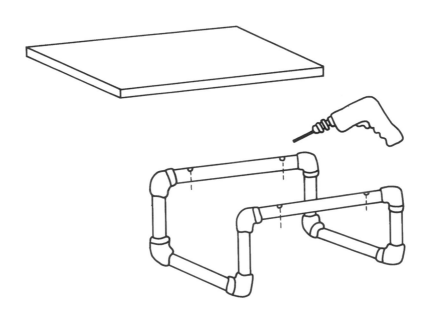

Children's Folk Art

Materials needed:

Child's artwork
1-inch thick pine board (large enough to fit draw-
    ing)
Opaque projector, carbon paper, sewer's tracing
    wheel
Acrylic paints
Paintbrushes
Scrap wood (dowels, cubes, and so forth) for creat-
    ing stands for artwork
Clear, non-yellowing finish
Coping saw (band saw if possible)

Step 1: Paint board the same color as the back-
ground color of the artwork.

Step 2: Transfer artwork onto the painted board with a pencil (use opaque projector,
carbon paper, or tracing wheel).

Step 3: Cut out the shape of the design with a coping saw (or band saw if possible).

Step 4: Paint the wood, duplicating as closely as possible your child's brush strokes,
colors, and mistakes. (This should be a keepsake of your child's artwork, not your own—
although you can make your own, too.)

Step 5: Create a stand for the cutout by doing *one* of the following:
(A) Drill a hole in the bottom of the cutout and a scrap of wood. Hot glue a dowel
     (any length) between the two and paint. You may want to hot glue the scrap of
     wood to a larger, painted base for additional support.

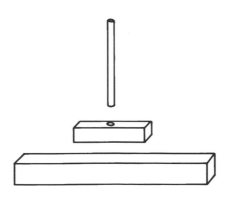

(B)   Hot glue the cutout directly to a larger, painted base.

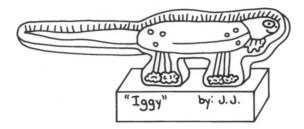

(C)   Hot glue a painted scrap of wood, vertically, to the back of the cutout, so it stands up like a picture frame.

Step 6: Seal the artwork with a clear finish. Let dry and enjoy! These look great on the mantel or any bookshelf.

5

"It's the Day
We Get Ready
for Sunday"

"It's the Day We Get Ready for Sunday"

The "Sunday Box" is a special box filled with games and activities especially suited for Sunday—although you should encourage your children to use the box whenever they like. A friend gave a Sunday Box to my family one Christmas and we love it; I hope you will too. These games also serve as great last-minute family home evening activities.

Kept in a storage box, a cardboard tote, and old suitcase, or even a file cabinet, these games and activities will last a long time. I have included ten of my favorites in this chapter:

1. Mormon Bingo

2. Count Your Blessings

3. Cookie Sheet Stories

4. Bible Bingo

5. Old Prophets

6. Fish for Prophets

7. Concentration

8. Mormonary

9. Family Journal

10. Gospel Puzzles

Mormon Bingo

The object of the game: Try to be the first to cover up five pictures in a row (up and down, across, or diagonal) with your playing pieces.

How to play: Give every player his/her own unique playing card from the following pages and twenty-five playing pieces; you can use beans, coins, candy, or even cut-up squares of paper.

Have Mom or Dad read stories out of the *Friend*, the *New Era*, or the *Ensign*. Cover up the pictures on your card as soon as you hear the word or phrase they represent. For example, when they read the prophet's words, "It is important to read the Book of Mormon," you can put a playing piece over the square that contains a picture of the Book of Mormon.

CHURCH	BOOK OF MORMON	HOME	PRAYER	JOURNAL
MUSIC	SACRAMENT	PROPHETS	MISSIONARY	PIONEERS
JESUS	COMMANDMENTS	FREE	FAMILY	TEMPLE
MARRIAGE	TIME	LOVE	TITHING	FAITH
WORD OF WISDOM	BIBLE	WORK	GENEALOGY	FAMILY HOME EVENING

MARRIAGE	COMMANDMENTS	MISSIONARY	CHURCH	TITHING
LOVE	WORK	GENEALOGY	PRAYER	JESUS
TIME	HOME	FREE	FAITH	BIBLE
BOOK OF MORMON	FAMILY	PIONEERS	SACRAMENT	WORD OF WISDOM
TEMPLE	PROPHETS	FAMILY HOME EVENING	MUSIC	JOURNAL

BIBLE	FAITH	FAMILY	HOME	LOVE
SACRAMENT	FAMILY HOME EVENING	TIME	MARRIAGE	WORK
PROPHETS	MISSIONARY	FREE	PRAYER	PIONEERS
CHURCH	JOURNAL	BOOK OF MORMON	TEMPLE	JESUS
MUSIC	GENEALOGY	COMMANDMENTS	WORDS OF WISDOM	TITHING

PIONEERS	WORDS OF WISDOM	FAMILY HOME EVENING	PROPHETS	TIME
WORK	JOURNAL	JESUS	HOME	BOOK OF MORMON
FAITH	BIBLE	FREE	COMMANDMENTS	FAMILY
GENEALOGY	LOVE	TEMPLE	MISSIONARY	MUSIC
CHURCH	TITHING	PRAYER	MARRIAGE	SACRAMENT

PROPHETS	TITHING	FAITH	LOVE	TIME
JOURNAL	TEMPLE	PRAYER	MUSIC	WORDS OF WISDOM
SACRAMENT	FAMILY	FREE	JESUS	FAMILY HOME EVENING
COMMANDMENTS	WORK	CHURCH	HOME	GENEALOGY
MISSIONARY	BIBLE	MARRIAGE	BOOK OF MORMON	PIONEERS

Count Your Blessings

Object of the game: Try to make it to the finish line first.

Set up: Borrow one die from another board game in your games closet, copy and cut out the draw cards from the following pages, and carefully remove the two sections of the game board from pages 103 and 105 in the book and tape together. (The game will last longer if you laminate the playing pieces.) Set the cards face down in a stack.

How to play: The youngest goes first, and play moves clockwise. Roll the die and move the number of spaces that you roll. If you land on a smiling face, you must name one of your blessings. If you can't do it, you have to go back to the last space you occupied. If you land on a "Pick a card" space, you need to draw a card and do what it says. If you can't do what it tells you to do, you have to go back to the last space you occupied. If you land on a "Go ahead" or "Go back" space, follow that direction first, and then do whatever is required on your new space. Again, if you can't follow that direction, you must go back to the space you occupied *before* landing on the "Go ahead" or "Go back" space.

Variation 1: When you land on a smiling face you must name as many blessings as the number you rolled. For example, if you roll a three and land on a smiling face, you must name three blessings in order to remain on that space.

Variation 2: Put a time limit on each turn; anywhere from five seconds for older players to fifteen seconds for the little ones will work well.

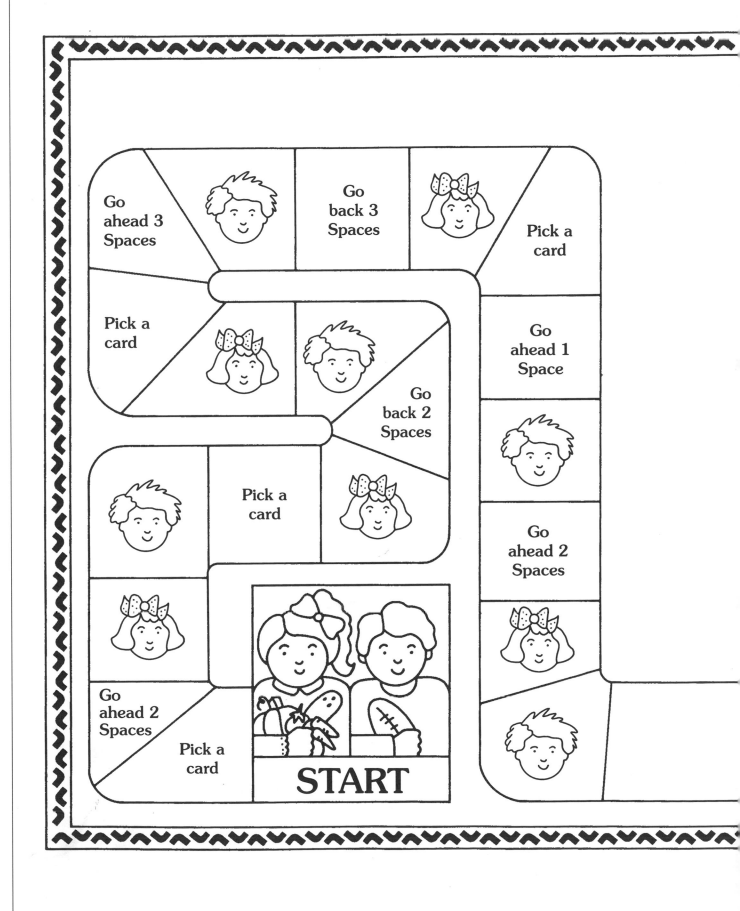

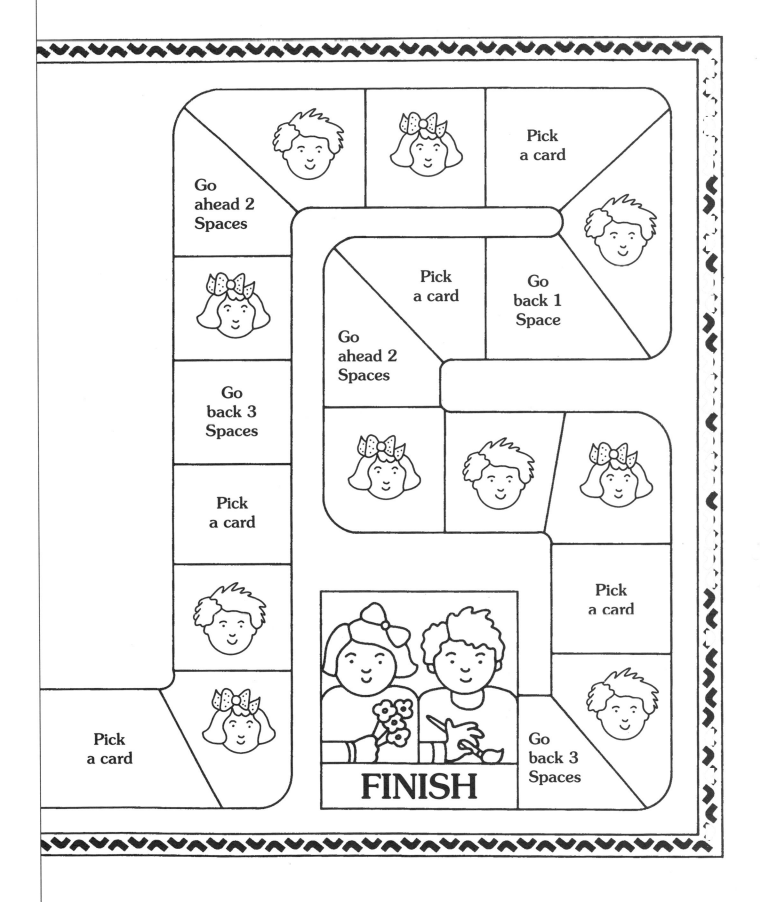

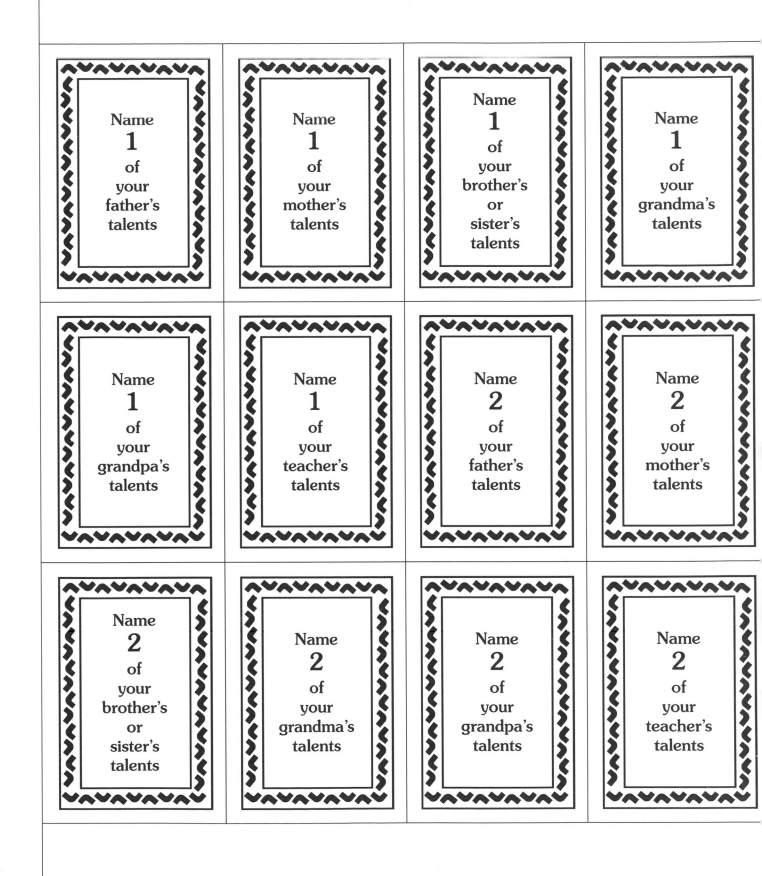

Name
1
of
your
father's
talents

Name
1
of
your
mother's
talents

Name
1
of
your
brother's
or
sister's
talents

Name
1
of
your
grandma's
talents

Name
1
of
your
grandpa's
talents

Name
1
of
your
teacher's
talents

Name
2
of
your
father's
talents

Name
2
of
your
mother's
talents

Name
2
of
your
brother's
or
sister's
talents

Name
2
of
your
grandma's
talents

Name
2
of
your
grandpa's
talents

Name
2
of
your
teacher's
talents

Name a person who has been a blessing in your life

Name a person who has been a blessing in your life

Name a person who has been a blessing in your life

Name a person who has been a blessing in your life

Name a person who has been a blessing in your life

Name a person who has been a blessing in your life

Name a person who has been a blessing in your life

Name a person who has been a blessing in your life

Name a place that has been a blessing in your life

Name a place that has been a blessing in your life

Name a place that has been a blessing in your life

Name a place that has been a blessing in your life

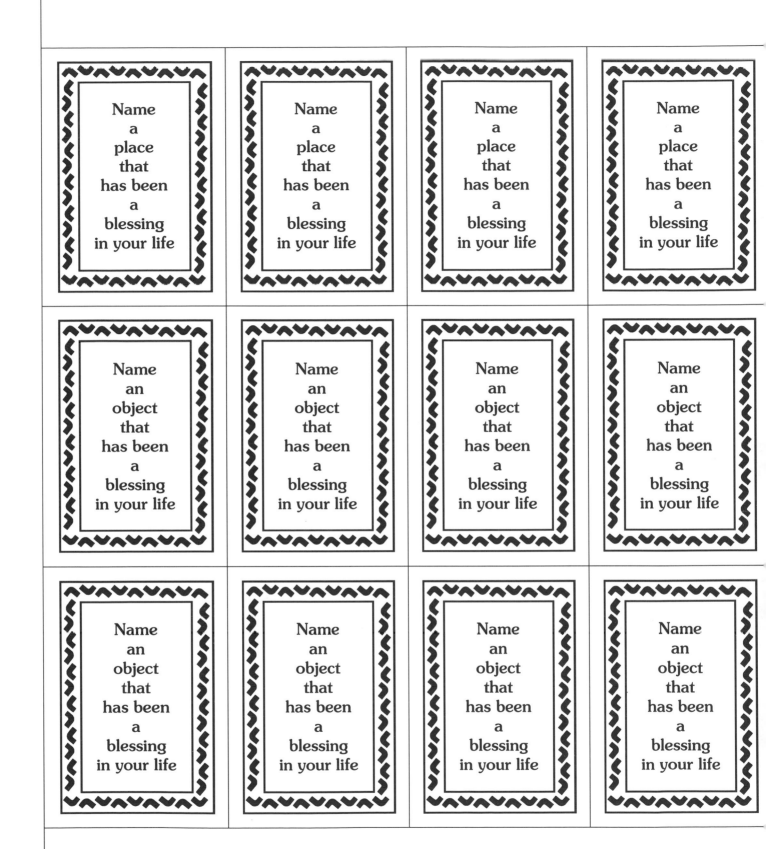

Name
a
place
that
has been
a
blessing
in your life

Name
a
place
that
has been
a
blessing
in your life

Name
a
place
that
has been
a
blessing
in your life

Name
a
place
that
has been
a
blessing
in your life

Name
an
object
that
has been
a
blessing
in your life

Name
an
object
that
has been
a
blessing
in your life

Name
an
object
that
has been
a
blessing
in your life

Name
an
object
that
has been
a
blessing
in your life

Name
an
object
that
has been
a
blessing
in your life

Name
an
object
that
has been
a
blessing
in your life

Name
an
object
that
has been
a
blessing
in your life

Name
an
object
that
has been
a
blessing
in your life

Cookie Sheet Stories

Object of activity: To have fun creating unusual stories using magnetic pictures you "hold up" on an ordinary cookie sheet.

How to do it: Label five plastic zippered storage bags: *Person, Place, Name, Animal,* and *Thing.* Search magazines for pictures that match the accompanying picture bag suggestions, or draw your own. Cut the pictures out and label them. Then laminate the pictures or glue them to cardstock. To make the pictures stick to the cookie sheet, affix a small piece of magnetic tape to the back of each one. Place the pictures in their corresponding picture bags.

Now you are ready to tell your story. I have included three stories to get you started. Read the story as it is written; but, when you come to a blank (thing, for example), pull a picture out of the bag that the blank calls for, and set it on the cookie sheet. When you come to a blank that also includes a number (thing 2, for example), you will know that that particular picture will be used again in the story. (When you come to another thing 2 blank, you will say and point to the same picture as you did the first time.)

Try using stories from the *Friend* magazine, too. When you come to a person, place, name, animal, or thing, simply substitute the pictures in your picture bags for those items and tell your silly story.

This can be a fun activity even *without* the pictures. Still label five bags; but, instead of placing pictures inside, simply use the word strips on pp. 115-119. Place each word strip into the appropriate bag and *tell* the story.

You can also make stories up as you go, using your own imagination and the pictures in your bags (or using wordstrips—both ways are lots of fun).

Picture Bag Suggestions

Person:
Mom
Son
Man
Monster
Woman
Mailman
Girl
Boy
Father

Name:
Goldilocks
Peter
Rumpelstiltskin
Mr. Ed
Lucy
Mergutroid
Captain Kangaroo
Annie

Place:
Germany
Town
England
Big world
Grocery store
Forest
Beach
Hawaii
Candy store

Animal:
Pig
Bear
Wolf
Goose
Cow
Rabbit
Kitten
Dog
Raccoon
Elephant

Thing:
Snack
Door
Chimney
Roof
Celery
Carrot
Eggs
Seed
Moon
Window
Beanstalk
Diamonds
Potatoes
Cottage
Table
Bed
Money
Milk
Rubies
Stick
Food

Person	Place
Mom	Germany
Son	Town
Man	England
Monster	Big world
Woman	Grocery store
Mailman	Forest
Girl	Beach
Boy	Hawaii
Father	Candy store

Name	Animal
Goldilocks	Pig
Peter	Bear
Rumpelstiltskin	Wolf
Mr. Ed	Goose
Lucy	Cow
Mergutroid	Rabbit
Captain Kangaroo	Kitten
Annie	Dog
	Raccoon
	Elephant

Thing	
Snack	Diamonds
Door	Potatoes
Chimney	Cottage
Roof	Table
Celery	Bed
Carrot	Money
Eggs	Milk
Seed	Rubies
Moon	Stick
Window	Food
Beanstalk	

Story 1

Once upon a time there was a <u>person 1</u> and <u>person 2</u>, named <u>name 1</u>, who lived in <u>place 1</u>. They were very poor. They owned a tiny, one-room <u>thing</u>, a <u>thing</u>, and a <u>animal 1</u>. To earn <u>thing 1</u> for food, they sold the <u>thing 2</u> from their <u>animal 1</u>. One day, however, the <u>animal 1</u>'s <u>thing 2</u> went dry and they needed to sell the <u>animal 1</u> to have enough <u>thing 1</u> for food. This was a sad day, because they loved their <u>animal 1</u>.

<u>Name 1</u>, took the <u>animal 1</u> into <u>place</u> to sell her, and on the way ran into a funny looking <u>person</u> named <u>name 2</u>. He/She told <u>name 1</u> a fantastic story about a castle in the clouds. In that castle was a <u>animal 2</u> that laid golden <u>thing 3</u>s. <u>Name 2</u> told <u>name 1</u> that if he/she could get his/her hands on this, he/she and his/her <u>person 1</u> would be the richest in all of <u>place 1</u>. All <u>name 1</u> needed to do was give <u>name 2</u> the <u>animal 1</u>, and he/she would give <u>name 1</u> a <u>thing 4</u> in return—a magic <u>thing 4</u>.

<u>Name 2</u> told <u>name 1</u> that if he/she planted the <u>thing 4</u> under a full <u>thing</u>, it would grow so big and tall that he/she would be able to climb it to the castle in the clouds and bring the <u>animal 2</u> home with him/her. That sounded wonderful to <u>name 1</u>. So he/she made the trade and ran home to tell his/her <u>person 1</u> the good news.

Unfortunately for <u>name 1</u>, his/her <u>person 1</u> didn't think it was such good news at all. In fact, he/she became angry with <u>name 1</u>; he/she sent him to his/her <u>thing</u> and threw the <u>thing 4</u> out the <u>thing</u>. That evening, while everyone was sleeping, the <u>thing 4</u> grew into a huge <u>thing 5</u>.

<u>Name 1</u> awoke early the next morning and found the <u>thing 5</u>. Immediately, he/she began to climb it. It took a long time. As he/she broke through the top of the clouds he/she saw a beautiful castle adorned with <u>thing</u> and <u>thing</u>. As he/she walked up to it, he/she found that it was bigger than he thought—so big, in fact, that he/she could walk right under the front door—which he/she did.

After a lot of searching, he/she did find the <u>animal 2</u>. But, it was on the stomach of a sleeping giant <u>person 3</u>, thirty feet tall. <u>Name 2</u> forgot to tell <u>name 1</u> about this. He/she was afraid and almost turned back, but the <u>animal 2</u> whispered, "Please, rescue me. The <u>person 3</u> is keeping me here as his prisoner—please!"

The <u>person 3</u>'s stomach was a long way off the ground, so <u>name 1</u> found a long <u>thing 6</u> that just reached the <u>animal 2</u>. Quietly, he/she said, "Grab onto the <u>thing 6</u>, and I will lift you off." The <u>animal 2</u> did grab onto the <u>thing 6</u>, and <u>name 1</u> did lift her off, but the <u>thing 6</u> fell to the ground with such a bang that the <u>person 3</u> woke up.

The <u>person 3</u> saw <u>name 1</u> running with the <u>animal 2</u> and started to chase them. Just as the <u>person 3</u> caught up with <u>name 1</u> and the <u>animal 2</u>, <u>name 1</u> landed safely on the ground, he/she chopped down the <u>thing 5</u> to be sure that the <u>person 3</u> wouldn't follow them. The

animal 2 was so grateful to name 1 for rescuing her that she laid a thousand golden thing 3s for him/her and then flew away to find her family.

Name 1 and his/her person 1 would never again have to worry about having enough thing to eat.

Story 2

Once upon a time there were three animal 1s. They lived in a cute little thing 1 in the woods of place. One day, they went for a walk. While they were gone a cute little person 1 named name 1 wandered by who saw their little thing 1. She [use "he" or "she"—whichever seems to fit—for this character from this point on] was very hungry so she knocked at the thing 2, hoping that someone would answer and offer her a thing to eat.

Nobody answered the front thing 2, so she went to try the back thing 2. When she went to knock, she found that it was already opened. So, she let herself in. As she walked inside, she saw three bowls of thing 3 on the table and decided to try it. The first one was too hot. The second one was too cold. But the third one was just right, and she drank it all up.

After eating the thing 3, she was so full that she needed to sit down for a while. She saw three thing 4s. One was big and hard, another was too soft, and the third was just perfect. So, she sat down—and it broke! It broke into a hundred pieces.

She still needed to rest after that delicious meal, so she went upstairs, looking for another place to sit. And she found something even better; she found three thing 5s. One was too hard, the other was too soft, but the third was just right. So, she decided to lie down on it. It was so comfortable that she fell asleep instantly.

Moments later, the three animal 1s returned home to find their thing 3 eaten and a thing 4 broken. They went upstairs to see if anything else was missing or broken. Instead, they found a little person 1 sleeping in one of their thing 5s. Name 1 woke up to find three animal 1s looking at her. She was very scared and ran out of the thing 1.

The animal 1s followed her, told her that everything was all right and that they wanted to be her friends. They all lived happily ever after.

Story 3

Once upon a time there were three little animal 1s who all lived together with their person and person. The oldest was very sensible and wise. The other two were very foolish. One day they all decided to go out into place and build homes of their own.

The youngest <u>animal 1</u> built a house out of <u>thing 1</u> and the middle <u>animal 1</u> built his out of <u>thing 2</u>. But, the oldest <u>animal 1</u>, being the wise one, built his out of <u>thing 3</u> so that it would stand up to bad weather and a big bad <u>animal 2</u>.

One day, as the youngest <u>animal 1</u> was watching <u>thing</u> in his house of <u>thing 1</u>, a big bad <u>animal 2</u> did come to the door and say, "Little <u>animal 1</u>, little <u>animal 1</u>, let me come in."

The <u>animal 1</u> replied, "Not by the hair of my chinny chin chin."

"Then I'll huff and I'll puff and I'll blow your house in!" And that he did. The little <u>animal 1</u> ran as fast as he could to his middle brother's <u>thing 2</u> house, quickly got inside, and locked the door.

The <u>animal 2</u> knocked at the door and said, "Little <u>animal 1</u>s, little <u>animal 1</u>s, let me come in."

"Not by the hair of our chinny chin chins," said the two <u>animal 1</u>s inside.

The <u>animal 2</u> shouted, "Then I'll huff and I'll puff and I'll blow your house in!" And again, he did as he said and the two little <u>animal 1</u>s scrambled to reach their oldest brother's house before the <u>animal 2</u> could catch them.

Feeling pretty confident by now, the <u>animal 2</u> was sure that he was about to have a delicious dinner of <u>animal 1</u>, <u>thing</u>, <u>thing</u>, and <u>thing</u>. He said, "Little <u>animal 1</u>s, little <u>animal 1</u>s, let me come in."

"Not by the hairs on our chinny chin chins," said the <u>animal 1</u>s.

"Then I'll huff and I'll puff and I'll blow your house in!" said the <u>animal 2</u>. And he did huff and puff. But this time, the house didn't blow down. So he tried again. Still, the house remained standing. So, he decided that he would outsmart the <u>animal 1</u>s and climb down their <u>thing 4</u>.

The <u>animal 1</u>s saw the <u>animal 2</u> climbing onto their <u>thing 5</u> and suspected that he might try to climb down their <u>thing 4</u>. So, they lit a fire and set a big pot of <u>thing 6</u> on it to boil. When the <u>animal 2</u> jumped down their <u>thing 4</u> and landed into their boiling pot of <u>thing 6</u>, they quickly put the cover on the pot and made a wonderful <u>animal 2</u> soup, complete with <u>thing</u>, <u>thing</u>, and <u>thing</u>.

After dinner, the two younger <u>animal 1</u>s rebuilt their houses. And can you guess what they built them out of? That's right—<u>thing 3</u>.

Bible Bingo

The object of the game: Try to be the first to cover up five pictures in a row (up and down, across, or diagonal) with your playing pieces.

How to play: Give every player their own unique playing card from the following pages and twenty-five playing pieces; you can use beans, coins, candy, or even cut-up squares of paper.

Cut out the clues from the Clue Sheet provided, fold each one, and put them into a bowl. Take turns drawing and reading the clues. When a player sees an answer to a clue he can cover up the answer on his card with a playing piece. Play continues until one person has a row of five consecutive squares covered and yells, "Bingo."

DAVID	OIL	NUMBERS	ANIMALS	PRAYER
HEARTS	JERICHO	DOVE	FORTY	LITTLE CHILDREN
HOUSE	TWO	FREE	CHURCH	MOSES
HOLY GHOST	GARDEN OF GETHSEMANE	SCRIPTURES	SHEEP	MANGER
ARK	TALENTS	MARY	DANIEL	ABRAHAM

MOSES	SHEEP	ABRAHAM	MARY	HEARTS
ADAM	ARK	DOVE	OIL	EVE
MANGER	PRAYER	FREE	TALENTS	FORTY
TWELVE	JERICHO	SCRIPTURES	DANIEL	MAN
DAVID	ANIMALS	MATTHEW	CHURCH	JOHN THE BAPTIST

MANGER	JOHN THE BAPTIST	TWELVE	DANIEL	GARDEN OF GETHSEMANE
PRAYER	TWO	MOSES	ARK	SHEEP
TALENTS	ANIMALS	FREE	HOUSE	DOVE
OIL	ADAM	HEARTS	MATTHEW	JERICHO
LITTLE CHILDREN	ABRAHAM	NUMBERS	MARY	EVE

DANIEL	MATTHEW	DAVID	TALENTS	SCRIPTURES
MAN	ADAM	HEARTS	EVE	TWELVE
FORTY	ARK	FREE	MOSES	GARDEN OF GETHSEMANE
ABRAHAM	CHURCH	HOLY GHOST	HOUSE	NUMBERS
ANIMALS	SHEEP	PRAYER	LITTLE CHILDREN	JOHN THE BAPTIST

JOHN THE BAPTIST	CHURCH	DANIEL	HOLY GHOST	MOSES
TALENTS	GARDEN OF GETHSEMANE	DOVE	ARK	LITTLE CHILDREN
MANGER	HOUSE	FREE	PRAYER	SHEEP
ADAM	NUMBERS	MARY	JERICHO	ANIMALS
TWO	HEARTS	OIL	MAN	MATTHEW

MANGER	ADAM	ARK	HEARTS	LITTLE CHILDREN
DOVE	DANIEL	HOUSE	MAN	OIL
CHURCH	ABRAHAM	FREE	MOSES	EVE
HOLY GHOST	SHEEP	ANIMALS	MATTHEW	JERICHO
NUMBERS	GARDEN OF GETHSEMANE	TALENTS	MARY	JOHN THE BAPTIST

Clue Sheet

1. Which prophet was involved with parting the Red Sea?
Moses

2. How many days and nights did Jesus fast in the wilderness?
Forty

3. The first mortals to inhabit the earth were Adam and _____ .
Eve

4. What did the prophet Noah build?
An Ark

5. What did the prophet Noah fill his ark with?
Animals

6. We are commanded to love the Lord our God with all our _____.
Hearts

7. _____ slew the giant Goliath.
David

8. _____ and the lions' den.
   Daniel

9. Who wrote the first book in the New Testament?
   Matthew

10. Who baptized Jesus?
    John the Baptist

11. What city was destroyed by trumpets?
    Jericho

12. How can we talk to Heavenly Father?
    Prayer

13. We are commanded to go to _____ on Sunday.
    Church

14. Five of the ten virgins had plenty of this in their lamps.
    Oil

15. You had better not hide these under a bushel.
    Talents

16. Jesus was born in a _____.
Manger

17. Jesus had how many Apostles?
Twelve

18. What was the name of Jesus' mother?
Mary

19. Jesus said, "Suffer the _____ to come unto me."
Little Children

20. Who is known as the "father of many nations"?
Abraham

21. In which garden did Jesus pray the day before He was crucified?
The Garden of Gethsemane

22. He is also known as the Comforter.
The Holy Ghost

23. When Jesus appeared to the disciples at the sea of Tiberias,
He said, "Feed my _____."
Sheep

24. We can gain a testimony of Jesus Christ through reading the _____.
Scriptures

25. Who was Eve's husband?
Adam

26. When Jesus was baptized, the Holy Ghost descended in the sign of a _____.
Dove

27. How many of each kind of animal boarded Noah's ark?
Two

28. Psalm 118:8 says, "It is better to trust in the Lord than
to put confidence in _____."
Man

29. Joshua 24:15 says, ". . . choose you this day whom ye will serve; . . . but as
for me and my _____, we will serve the Lord."
House

30. The fourth book in the Old Testament is _____.
Numbers

Old Prophets (similar to Old Maid)

Object of the game: Try to be the first to find a match for all of the cards in your hand.

How to play: Make two copies of all of the prophets cards (found later in this chapter) onto cardstock-weight paper; then color them, cut them out, and if desired, laminate them. (You can use clear contact paper instead of actually laminating them; it is less expensive and easy to do yourself).

This game works best if played with two to four players. First, deal all of the cards. Before play begins, each player takes a turn to *name* and set down on the game table any matches he/she might have (the idea is to become more familiar with our modern-day prophets).

Now you're ready to begin playing. Start with the player to the dealer's left and move clockwise. Each player chooses a card out of the next player's deck, hoping for a match. If it matches, the pair can be *named* and placed on the table. If it doesn't match, it simply becomes part of the player's hand. Play continues this way until someone matches all of the cards in his hand.

Fish for Prophets (similar to Go Fish)

Object of the game: Try to be the first one to set down all of the cards in your hand.

How to play: Make four copies of all of the prophets cards (found later in this chapter) onto cardstock-weight paper; then color them, cut them out, and laminate them if desired (or just use clear contact paper).

This game works best if played with two to four players. First, deal seven cards to each player and set the rest in a pile within everyone's reach. Play moves clockwise, and the player to dealer's left begins. During each turn, players can ask any person for any card. If the person has the card, he must give it up.

The turn continues until the player asks for a card that a person doesn't have, at which time the person says, "Go fish!" The player then draws a card from the pile and it becomes the next player's turn. However, if the card drawn from the pile is the same one the player just asked for, the player says, "Fish, fish, I got my wish" and continues playing until the turn is over.

When a player accumulates four-of-a-kind he can place them on the table. The winner is the first one to have no cards in his hand.

Concentration (using the prophets cards)

Object of the game: Try to earn the most cards by making the most matches.

How to play: Make two copies of each of the prophets cards (found later in this chapter) onto cardstock-weight paper. Then color them, cut them out, and laminate them if desired (or use clear contact paper). Mix up the cards and place them all face down on a table in grid fashion.

Players take turns turning over two cards. When a match is made, the player can keep the match *if* he remembers to *name* the prophet. Each turn continues until the two cards that are turned over do not match; then it's the next player's turn. The one who earns the most cards wins.

Prophets Cards

Joseph Smith

Brigham Young

John Taylor

Wilford Woodruff

Lorenzo Snow

Joseph F. Smith

Heber J. Grant

George Albert Smith

David O. McKay

Joseph Fielding Smith

Harold B. Lee

Spencer W. Kimball

Ezra Taft Benson

Mormonary (similar to Pictionary)

The object of the game: Try to earn more points than the opposing team by guessing what your teammates draw before the time runs out.

How to play: Gather together the following items:

1. A dry erasable board with a marker, a chalkboard with chalk, or a large pad of paper with a marker.
2. The Mormonary cards from the following pages copied onto cardstock-weight paper and laminated (if desired).
3. A pad of paper and pencil for scoring.
4. A timing device (such as an egg timer).

First, divide into teams. The first team chooses a player to draw. That player selects a card and tries to draw a picture within the allotted time (one minute is good) that will help his teammates guess the scripture story or the song (songs are from the hymnbook and the *Children's Songbook*) written on the card.

If the team guesses the right answer, they get a point. Then it is the second team's turn. Play continues until each *team* has drawn five pictures *or* every member of both teams has had a chance to draw a picture (whichever number is greater). The team with the most points wins.

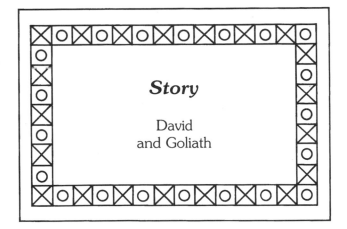

Story

David
and Goliath

Song

"Popcorn Popping"

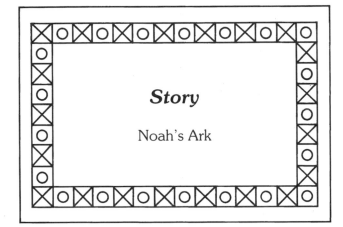

Story

Noah's Ark

Song

"Called to Serve"

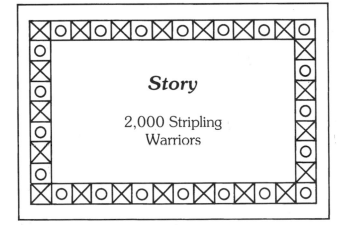

Story

2,000 Stripling
Warriors

Song

"Book of Mormon
Stories"

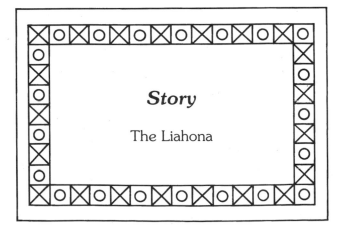

Story

The Liahona

Song

"Love at Home"

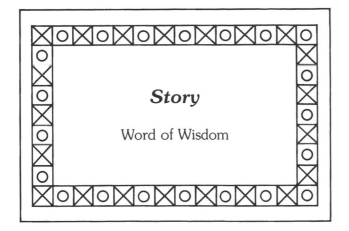

Story

Word of Wisdom

Song

"A Child's Prayer"

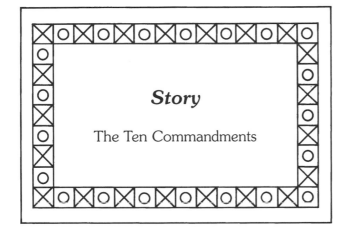

Story

The Ten Commandments

Song

"Teach Me to Walk
in the Light"

Story

Hearts of the
Children Turned to their Fathers

Song

"I Hope They
Call Me on a Mission"

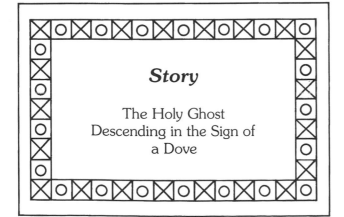

Story

The Holy Ghost
Descending in the Sign of
a Dove

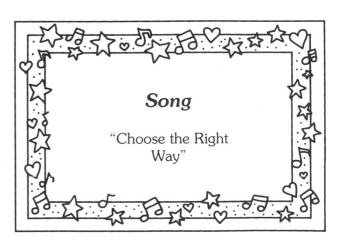

Song

"Choose the Right
Way"

Story

Hill Cumorah

Song

"I Have Two Little Hands"

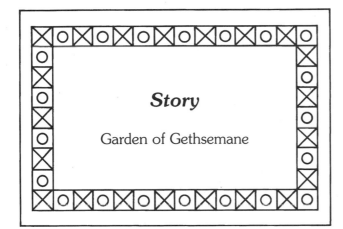

Story

Garden of Gethsemane

Song

"If You're Happy"

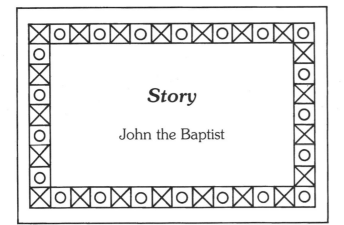

Story

John the Baptist

Song

"In the Leafy
Treetops"

Story

Daniel and
the Lions' Den

Song

"Pioneer Children Sang
As They Walked"

Story

The First Vision

Song

"I Am a Child of God"

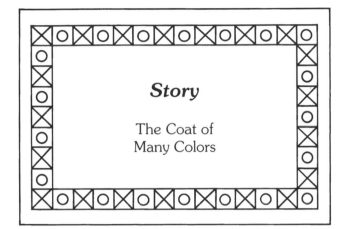

Story

The Coat of
Many Colors

Song

"Little Purple Pansies"

Story

The Tower of
Babel

Song

"Families Can
Be Together Forever"

Story

Cain and Abel

Song

"'Give,' Said the
Little Stream"

Family Journal

How to get started: Buy a loose-leaf notebook and label three dividers: Family Vacations, Special Occasions, and Daily Life. Each Sunday, give someone the responsibility of entering something in the Daily Life section of the journal. When the family goes on vacation or participates in another special event, such as a baptism, give everyone a sheet of paper and let them write their personal feelings about the occasion. Store the entries in the appropriate section of the journal.

Your family will love reading this journal in years to come.

Gospel Puzzles

How to get started: Buy several gospel pictures from a Church bookstore (or order them from the Church Distribution Center in Salt Lake City, Utah). Usually, these pictures are printed on stiff paper that works fine for puzzles. If your pictures are on thin paper, you will need to glue them to poster board to make them stiff enough to work with. (3M Spray Glue works great.)

Then, simply cut the pictures into puzzle shapes and store each one in its own plastic zippered storage bag.

About the Author

Deborah Sedgwick Stapley is a wife, homemaker, and mother of three who has devoted her entire adult life to finding innovative ways to manage home and family. Debbie's not embarrassed to tell people that she really loves her "work." That love, and her innate talent for performance, spawned her second (part-time) career: television.

She was discovered in 1990 by the producers of ABC Television's "HOME" Show. While looking for good homemaking tips to use on the show, they saw a video of Debbie describing several of her ideas. They initially invited her to appear as a guest on the show, and she has been a regular ever since. She now resolutely affirms that all of those years of giving talks in Primary and serving as the Homemaking Leader in Relief Society have really paid off.

In 1991, Debbie took a break from the show. During that break, she wrote this book and produced two "how-to" videos on craft ideas for the home, her forte. In addition to her home and television commitments she currently serves in her stake's Relief Society presidency and on the board of directors of the Arizona Children's Heart Fund. She also performs with a small singing group and is a popular speaker. She lives in Phoenix, Arizona, with her husband, Greg, and their three daughters.